יהי רצון שימלא
ה' כל משאלות
לבך לטובה

בברכה

This edition is dedicated in loving memory of

Stanley M. Klein

A man whose heartfelt compassion was matched only by the depths of his faith.

Harry and Rose Klein

Who together nurtured within their children and grandchildren a sense of love for one another and concern for our fellow man.

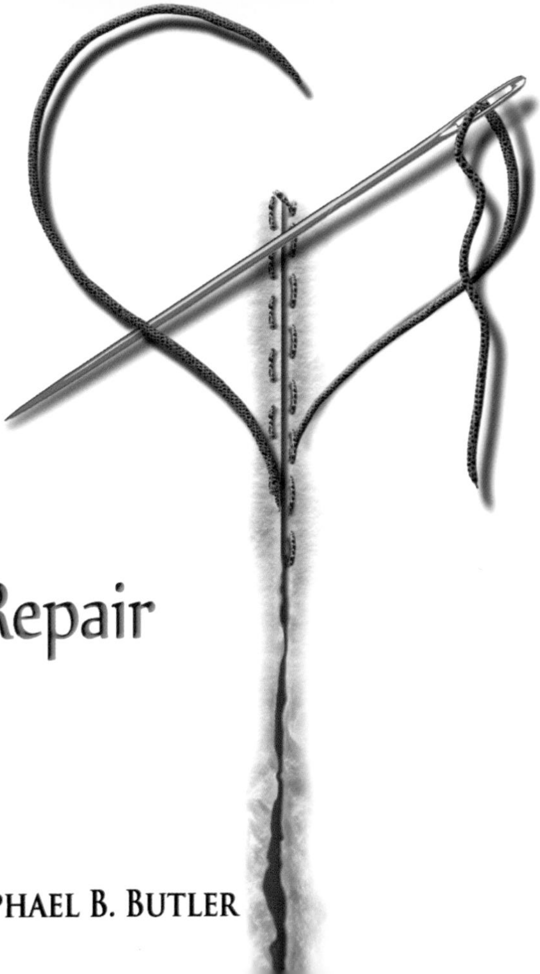

The Journey from Tear to Repair

RABBI RAPHAEL B. BUTLER

Special thanks to

Stanley Aaron Lebovic

Who has masterfully enhanced this work with his illustrative, graphic and literary contributions.

111 John Street / Suite 1720 / New York, NY 10038 / 212.791.7450

First Edition – First Impression / February 2015

Special thanks to The Judaica Press for graciously providing the English translation of[the Psalms.

ISBN 10: 1-60204-023-0 / ISBN 13: 978-1-60204-023-6

Printed in Canada by Kromar Printing

I dedicate this work to my dear father

Donald B. Butler of blessed memory

His towering presence and overwhelming influence
came from his constant devotion to God.

TABLE OF CONTENTS

PAGE 34

Is dedicated in honor of our treasured parents

DRS. FELIX AND MIRIAM GLAUBACH
DR. DAVID AND HARRIET BRYK

Is dedicated in memory of our beloved mother

DORIS BRYK ע״ה

Psalm 18 BRYK

Is dedicated in honor of our amazing children

DARREN AND AMANDA
BRADLEY, ANDREW AND SAMANTHA

By Tammy and Hillel Bryk

PAGE 38

Psalm 20 STEIN GELLER

Is dedicated in memory of our dear parents

DR. & MRS. STANLEY & CLARA EVANS
שמואל פנחס בן צבי הלוי ז״ל
חיה איטא בת הרב משה ע״ה

Whose vision was constantly focused on family and גמילת חסדים

Judi & Morse Geller, Marcie & Neil Stein and families

PAGE 42

Psalm 22 SCHULMAN

Is dedicated in memory of

ABRAHAM AND YETTA SCHULMAN ע״ה
Who began anew after the Shoah and merited to inspire their children, grandchildren and great grandchildren toward a life of devotion, service and faith.

By The Schulman family

PAGE 46

Psalm 23 SCHNALL

Is dedicated with tremendous gratitude

To our family, rabbanim, friends and כלל ישראל throughout the world who recited Tehillim on behalf of our children. ברוך אתה ה׳ שומע תפילה

Rena and Alan Schnall

PAGE 50

Psalm 28 KLEIN

Is dedicated in memory of

STANLEY M. KLEIN ז״ל
A man whose boundless compassion was matched only by the depths of his faith.

PAGE 54

Psalm 30 LEMBERG

Is dedicated in memory of

REB CHAIM BEN ZEV HACOHEN LEMBERG ז״ל
MALKA BAT TUVIA LEMBERG ע״ה
REB BARUCH BENDIT BEN NACHMAN ITZKOWITZ ז״ל
CHANA BAT YISRAEL CHAIM ITZKOWITZ ע״ה

By Danny and Blimy Lemberg

Psalm 31 SHEDLIN

Is dedicated in memory of

MILTON SHEDLIN ז"ל PAGE 58

A man of honesty, integrity and abiding faith. He celebrated in the accomplishments of our people and grieved in their despair.

Is dedicated in memory of our dear parents

HERMAN & ESTHER SEGAL ע"ה PAGE 62

חיים בן אברהם הלוי ז"ל

אסתר בת צבי אלימלך הכהן ע"ה

ERICH & ANNA WEINBERGER ע"ה

מרדכי בן יהודה הלוי ז"ל

חנה בת משה ע"ה

Psalm 32 SEGAL

Is dedicated in honor of our dear children

MATTHEW & ALLISON

By Alvin and Judith Segal

Psalm 33 LEBOVIC

Is dedicated in loving memory of

ALEX LEBOVIC ז"ל PAGE 66

His greatness was surpassed only by his humility.

By Stanley and Linda Lebovic

Psalm 37 NAYMARK

Is dedicated in memory of

DR. ABRAHAM AND RUTH NAYMARK ע"ה PAGE 70

Whose love of one another was matched only by their love for Medinat Yisrael and Am Yisrael.

Psalm 38 HARRIS

Is dedicated in loving memory of

JOSEPH DIAMOND ז"ל יוסף ב"ר יעקב צבי PAGE 74

May his memory be for a blessing.

יהי זכרו ברוך

By Lena and Richard Harris

Psalm 39 SCHMUTTER

Is dedicated to our dear parents

JACK GREENBLUM ז"ל AND MURIEL GREENBLUM PAGE 78

ZEV AND LISA SCHMUTTER ז"ל

By Irvin and Shelley Schmutter

PAGE 82

Psalm 49 BOBROW

Is dedicated in memory of our beloved grandparents

חנה רחל & יוסף אייזק ע״ה ANNIE & ISAAC MUSS
רבקה & שמואל ע״ה REBECCA & SAMUEL BOBROWITZ
אסתר לאה & זאב וולף ע״ה LILY & WOLF ISRAEL
שינדל & יעקב ע״ה JEANETTE & JACOB KRULL

By Julia and Norman Bobrow

PAGE 86

Psalm 56 RUBINFELD

Is dedicated for the continued refuah of

RUCHAMA SARA MIRYAM BEZALELY

By Teena and Stu Rubinfeld & Family

PAGE 90

Psalm 86 MARGOLIN

Is dedicated

IN MEMORY OF SEYMOUR MARGOLIN ז״ל
&
IN HONOR OF HELEN MARGOLIN

For their devotion to their family and their community.

By Howard, Debbie, Ari and Rachel Margolin

PAGE 94

Psalm 88 HOROWITZ

Is dedicated in loving memory of

MIKE NISSEL ז״ל,
JERRY AND MARTHA HOROWITZ ז״ל
IRVING AND SALLY SCHECHTER ז״ל
ZEV HOROWITZ ז״ל

By Sandy Nissel and Norman Horowitz & Rondi and Arthur Horowitz

PAGE 98

Psalm 89 SILVERSTEIN

We honor our dear parents

STANLEY AND RAINE SILVERSTEIN
Who have guided us with their lifelong example of devotion and love.

By Nina, Renee, Flori, Ami and Families

PAGE 102

Psalm 90 GETTENBERG

Is dedicated in memory of

לעילוי נשמת רחל אלכסנדרה ע״ה

By Dr. Chaim and Lynn Gettenberg

Psalm 91 AMINOV — Is dedicated in memory of

TSIVYA BAT RIVKA ע״ה
DAVID BEN RIVKA ז״ל
YAEL BAT MALKA ע״ה

PAGE 106

By Margarita and Lev Aminov

Psalm 102 SEPTIMUS — Is dedicated in memory of our dear parents

SEPTIMUS אליעזר צבי
SEPTIMUS חיה רחל
HIRTH שמואל פישל ודבורה

May their legacy of tzedakah and chesed continue to be an inspiration for all their descendants.

PAGE 110

By Bonnie and Barry Septimus

Psalm 103 GOTTLIEB — Is dedicated in memory of our beloved parents

RENEE' GOTTLIEB ע״ה
Beloved mother taken at an early age whose influence and memory lives on in our hearts forever.

JOSEPH HARCSZTARK ז״ל
Holocaust survivor and Palmach soldier
Beloved father and grandfather whose guidance is missed.

PAGE 114

By Deborah and Michael Gottlieb

Psalm 116 ENGEL — Is dedicated in honor of my dear parents

ARI BEN EUGENE ז״ל
Whose guiding hand is always felt.

LEAH BAT MARK

PAGE 118

By Jacqueline Engel

Psalm 118 HOCHBERG — Is dedicated in memory of

RABBI DR. HILLEL & GERTRUDE HOCHBERG ע״ה
MR. & MRS. JOSEPH & RUTH ULEVITCH ע״ה
May their precious legacy continue to inspire us and future generations.

PAGE 122

By Rabbi Shlomo and Karen Hochberg

Psalm 119 REZNIK — Is dedicated in memory of

BARRY DAVID REZNIK ע״ה
BETH REZNIK BELLER ע״ה
With love and understanding to all that find comfort in this meaningful book of Psalms.

PAGE 126

By Mrs. Eleanore Reznik, Children and Grandchildren

Psalm 121 MELTZER — Is generously sponsored by

LEVI & AHUVA MELTZER

PAGE 130

By Levi and Ahuva Meltzer

Psalm 142 HURWITZ | Is dedicated in memory of

ALLEN & REGINA HURWITZ ע״ה
אליהו בן שלמה הלוי ע״ה
רבקה בת אברהם שלמה ע״ה

PAGE 134

By Dr. and Mrs. David Hurwitz

Psalm 148 GOLDSTEIN | Is dedicated in honor of

BELA AND EMILIO GOLDSTEIN
EDITH AND ERIC HANAU

As an enduring z'chus for our dear parents, and in heartfelt tefillah for boundless nachas from our children and grandchildren.

PAGE 138

By Diane and Efraim Goldstein

א לַמְנַצֵּחַ בִּנְגִינוֹת
בְּאַפְּךָ תוֹכִיחֵנִי וּ

PSALMS
In Hebrew and English

PAGE 142

Acknowledgments & Encouragements

King David, in chronicling his Book of Psalms, underscores the principle that in every experience of life, 'God is my shadow'. A shadow that hovers and protects. A shadow that celebrates and grieves. Therefore, whether it be at moments of victory or defeat, the one consistent theme in the work of King David is that at any particular moment of time, God is present.

Of the one hundred and fifty various chapters in the Book of Psalms, at times of illness and crisis, we are directed toward specific psalms that shadow us in challenge and encourage us to find the expressive hand of God, even in despair. This brief work gives further voice to the messages of King David. Using various commentaries as our source, we have tried to integrate contemporary life experiences into the timeless messages of King David.

Through the artistry of Stan Lebovic, the essays come to life in a unique and masterful manner. We are grateful to Mr. Lebovic, not only for his original designs, but especially for the meaningful quotes of inspiration that accompany each design concept.

I thank MGG Willow, Bonnie Septimus, Karen Hochberg and Gitty Schachter, for their review of the manuscript, and their assistance in preparing it for publication.

Rabbi Meir Zlotowitz has been a guiding force in so many of the projects we have undertaken throughout the years. His ongoing legacy has shaped the searching Jewish world, and I am deeply appreciative of all his efforts to bring this work to fruition.

Most importantly, perhaps, is the Page of Reflections, wherein we all become writers, interpreting for ourselves in our own personal moment of challenge, how David's encouragement speaks to each one of us.

This work is designed to guide those who yearn for a closeness with God. That desire is, by definition, a process. Just as one cannot master a field of endeavor overnight, so too we are incapable of sustaining a nurturing bond with God without a sincere desire and sustained diligence. Once it clicks, we will find God as our Partner in our every endeavor. We will have discovered our Shadow and our Protector.

I dedicate this work to my dear father, Donald B. Butler of blessed memory, who lived his life with God as his shadow. It allowed him to appreciate his own potential, to be satisfied with his lot, to be a reservoir of care for others and a wellspring of boundless love for his family. I cannot honor my father without thanking God for the charmed life that my father and my dear mother, Chantze Butler, shared. It is my hope and prayer that God continues to be our mother's shadow, to care and protect her through her ensuing years of joy and pride in the family that she has nurtured.

And finally, in the words of King David, may God protect us in all our comings and goings, now and for eternity.

Rabbi Raphael B. Butler

The tear in the fabric of our reality is felt by every one of us. Its chasm so deep that our best efforts to simply grin and bear it only intensify the pain — widen the scope of our suffering.

The tear is relentless ... intentionally so.

Because the tear comes, not to afflict us, it comes to uplift us. It does not represent a defect, a blemish on our lives. While it cuts through the very heart of our being it does not define us. What defines us is what we make of the rip; how we choose to respond to the setback; how we manage to repair the tear.

In a Midrash in Breishis Rabba (39,3) Rav Brechiya quotes a verse from Shir HaShirim: "'*We have a little sister (achot) and she does not have breasts...*' (8:8) *We have a little sister, (achot)* – this refers to Avraham, who 'stitched together' (icha) all people of the earth. Bar Kapra said: Like one who stitches together a tear."

May these psalms and Rabbi Butler's beautiful elucidation of their intent, grant you the strength to succeed, the wisdom to realize that God has placed the needle and thread in your capable hands, and may He grant you the resolve to repair the tear like Avraham, one stitch at a time, until stitch by stitch, "all people of the earth" will be whole again.

Amen.

Stanley Aaron Lebovic

The
PSALMS
ELUCIDATED, ILLUMINATED AND REFLECTED UPON

Six

Psalm found on page 142

Among the many challenges we face in times of crisis, are the lack of perspective and the lack of hope. King David addresses these and other issues in this psalm. The psalm is full of words of anguish and distress, and describes endless tears. And yet, even at the moment when all seems to be lost, we implore God with the word *chaneini*, favor me. We beseech God to treat us with *chein*. Literally, *chein* means favor or grace. But the sages interpret it to refer to the kind of attention or favor that is undeserved — a *matnas chinam*, or an unearned gift. Thus, we plead with God for a kind of care or assistance that is not really deserved. And this is the essence of our request.

To offer such a plea in times of need and stress, one must have deep emotional strength and strong sense of faith. David implores us to appreciate that the God Who causes tears to flow, is the same compassionate God Who repairs, restores and heals.

In this psalm, David reflects that if suffering is a wake-up call for introspection, for repentance, and for a renewal of faith, we demonstrate those attributes as we express our thoughts, our doubts and our concerns, as we plead for God to rescind His decree.

The Radak suggests that when we offer this psalm with heartfelt fervor and supplication, we are assured that God will hear and respond to our prayers. God's response may not be the one we hope for — in fact, the response may be much different than what we expect — but we know that His response will be one that is appropriate for us. For God knows better than man what man needs and what will be of greatest benefit to him. We must therefore have true faith that God will treat us with *chein* – favor – even though we may not understand the treatment or even though the treatment may taste bitter. That unquestioning acceptance of God's decision is a true act of belief and faith.

Dedicated in honor of our dear parents
Edith Schlinsky, Rabbi Moish Schlinsky ז״ל & Frank and Klara Joseph ז״ל

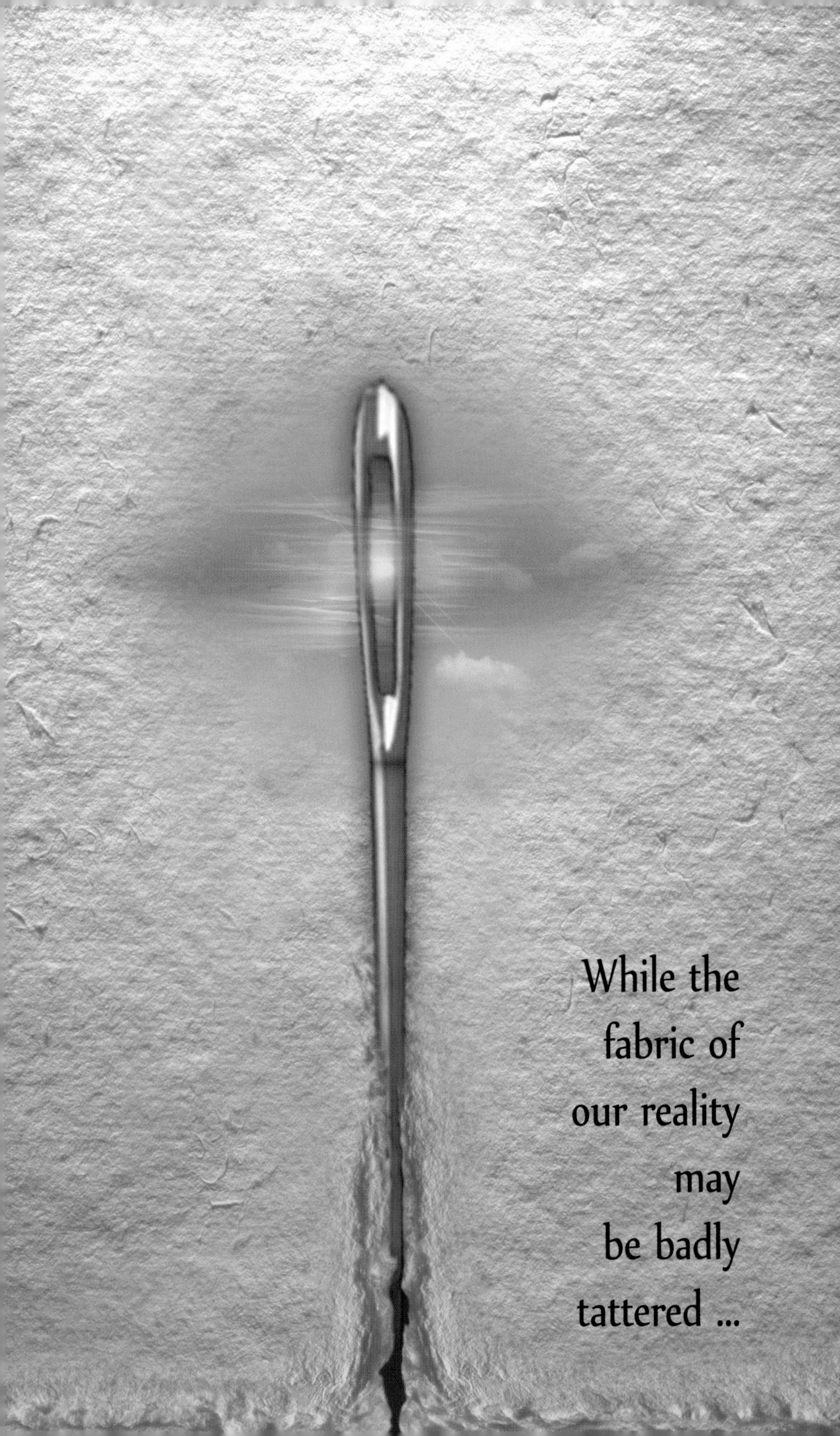
While the
fabric of
our reality
may
be badly
tattered ...

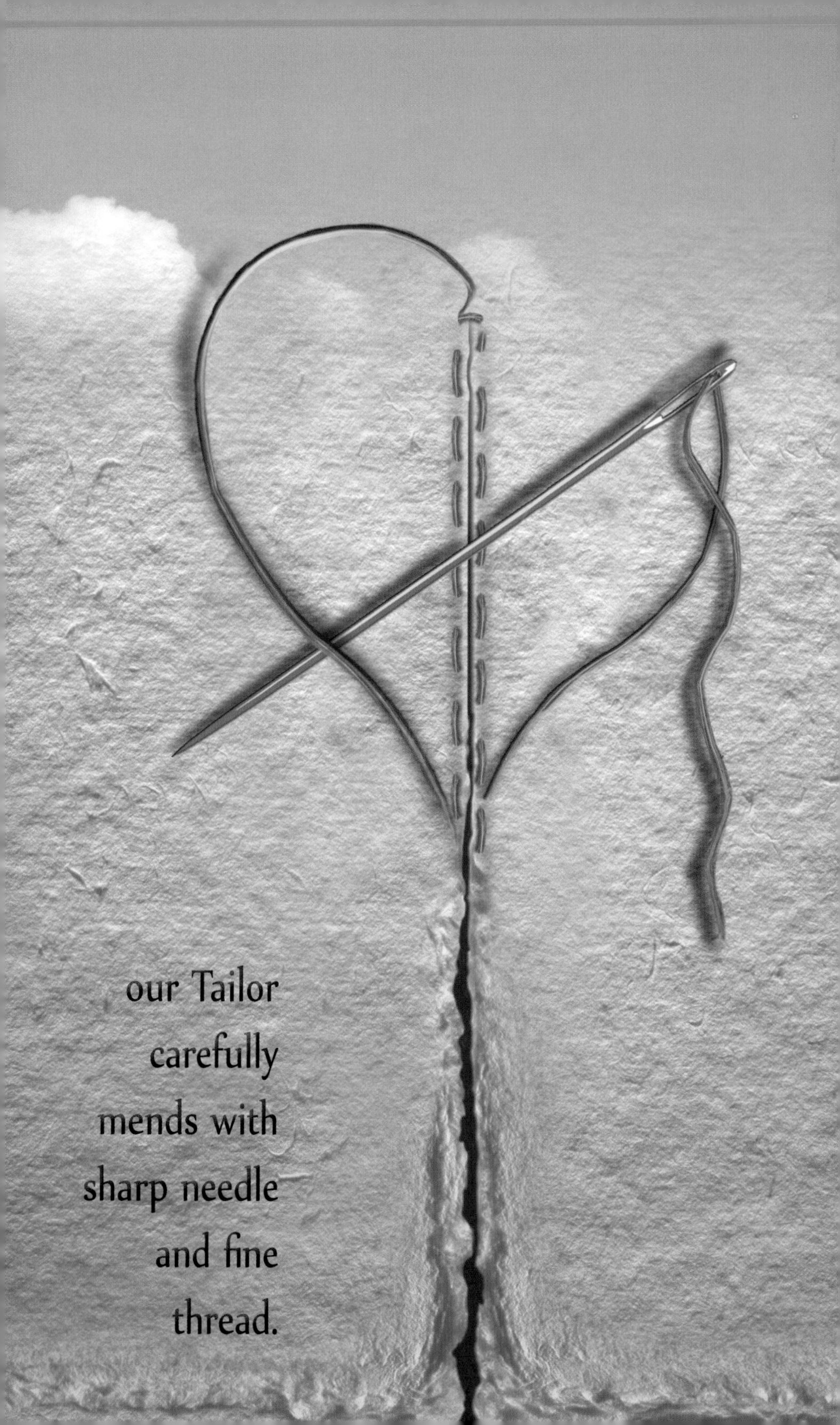

our Tailor
carefully
mends with
sharp needle
and fine
thread.

Reflections

While the fabric of our reality may be badly tattered . . .
our Tailor carefully mends with sharp needle and fine thread.

-SL-

Nine

Psalm found on page 142

One of the challenges we face in praying to God is creating a mindset devoid of any motive beyond the desire to bond with Him. In overcoming the vicissitudes of life, we often find ourselves asking for more and more while not expressing our appreciation for all of God's previous kindness.

At the start of this passage, David reminds us that we must separate the request for future assistance from the expressions of gratitude for all of God's past support; otherwise, our words would smack of insincerity, as if we recognize God's past goodness only as a means to ask for increasing benefits in the future. The *Chovos Halevavos* warns of the pitfalls of thanking God with an eye toward a future agenda rather than toward His sustenance to date. He posits that such a prayer of thanks lacks the essential requirement of a complete unrequited testimony of appreciation.

How difficult the moment of prayer becomes when we have such great needs for future help, yet are directed to first focus our full emphasis on God's past gifts of kindness. In this psalm, David frames the proper approach. We must begin with a full sincere expression of thanks, "With all my heart, I will proclaim all Your wondrous deeds," i.e., I pledge to glorify His Name irrespective of the future. Once I fulfill that pledge with full devotion, I may turn to God with my requests for future support.

Only by meditating upon God's infinite goodness, and thereby understanding that every breath, sound, and sight is a manifestation of His kindness, can a person say, "This is my God" — and look to Him for help in the future.

Dedicated in memory of
Jack Abroms ע״ה and Daniel Copans ע״ה

Hope in a
better
tomorrow
must not
blind us from
appreciating
the blessings
of today...

nor rob us
from
acknowledging
the splendor in
all our
yesterdays.

Reflections

Hope in a better tomorrow must not blind us from appreciating the blessings of today . . .

nor rob us from acknowledging the splendor in all our yesterdays.

-SL-

Thirteen

Psalm found on page 144

A feeling of abandonment can often make life's new challenges seem all the more daunting. When we perceive ourselves as disconnected from God and His lifeline of strength, life's imposing difficulties seem fearsome and insurmountable.

In this psalm, David offers an antidote by encouraging us to remain aggressively engaged in searching for resolution. He asks God to "enlighten my eyes" lest I pass on. Help me free myself from despair so that I can turn to a constructive search for solutions to my problems.

This is by no means a small request. While crisis may paralyze us, David urges us to keep probing and searching; maintain a positive equilibrium and look ahead toward a brighter tomorrow. It is neither the physical nor the emotional paralysis that David fears most. It is the fear of detachment from our spiritual bond with God. It is all too common in times of challenge to reach the conclusion that God has given up on us and we, therefore, give up on God.

David implores us to ask God for the enlightenment to awake our stoic soul, to rediscover our purpose in partnering with God in elevating His world. Partners in mission remain bonded in good times and bad. God, my partner in life, remains committed to me and me to Him.

Dedicated in honor of our dear children, grandchildren and great-grandchildren
The Teichman Family, Los Angeles, CA

It is the
mangled
unravel at
the end
of the
line ...

which reveals
the beginning
of possibilities.

Reflections

It is the mangled unravel at the end of the line ...
which reveals the beginning of possibilities.
-SL-

Sixteen

Psalm found on page 144

Our relationship with God and our dependence on Him evolves over a lifetime of thought and deed. The closer we mirror His image in our daily lives, the stronger the bond becomes. In this inspirational psalm, David explores the mindset required of a man of faith.

"I will bless Hashem Who has advised me, also in the nights my own intellect instructs me." How does God "advise" man? Although we are granted the opportunity to choose our own paths in life and every decision each and every day is ours to make, God is still actively advising us. Our challenge is to read those divine signs of advice. To many, they seem to be natural occurrences, but to the man of faith they are the hand of God, directing and advising His creations. To appreciate His presence and to follow His quiet instruction is the challenge of man. It is most appropriate, therefore, that when we offer words of prayer at times of challenge or at times of joy, we recognize the moment as a moment of "advice" — not of mere happenstance.

David offers probing advice on developing the sensitivity to appreciate the role of God within the construct of daily life. He suggests, "In the nights my own intellect instructs me." "Nights" represent both times of darkness and times of quiet, lonely introspection. When we quietly assess why events unfold as they do, and when we use our moments of quiet as opportunities for introspection, even our dark moments become meaningful.

David urges us to use such dark moments to find the instructive image of God. When tragedy occurs, he tells us, we should search for God's message, just as we should in times of joy. In fact, David reminds us, "I have set God before me always." To see God at all times and in all ways, requires that we use our quiet introspective moments for growth and inspiration.

Dedicated in honor of our dear children and families
Nina, Renee, Flori and Ami

WARNING
BRIDGE OUT
PROCEED WITH CAUTION

It is not
what the
signs
in life say ...

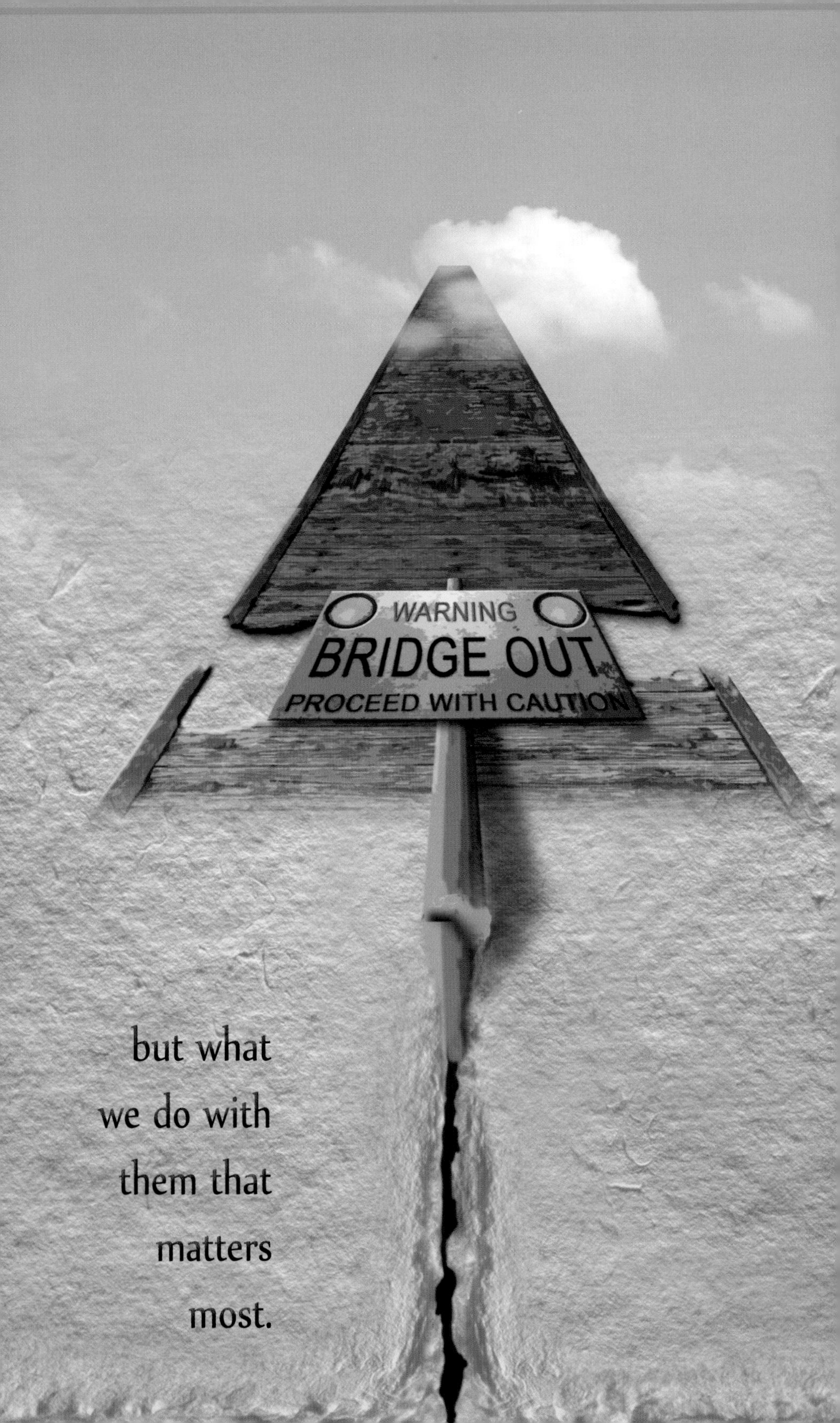
WARNING
BRIDGE OUT
PROCEED WITH CAUTION

but what
we do with
them that
matters
most.

Reflections

It is not what the signs in life say …
but what we do with them that matters most.
-SL-

Seventeen

Psalm found on page 146

The prospect of turning to God in prayer is an enriching one. It gives man the opportunity to unburden the soul with expressions of the heart — from the heart. In this psalm, David calls to mind an essential requisite of effective prayer. You must believe in both the process and ultimately, in the workings of God Himself.

"I have called out to You, because You will answer me, O God; incline Your ear to me, hear my utterances." We undertake the rigor of prayer not as an avenue to let off steam, but out of a deeply felt appreciation that God hears and responds to our deepest thoughts and needs. Oftentimes the momentary swirl of events prevents us from appreciating the intimacy of the exclusive personal relationship between God and man. We may believe that God directs the laws of nature — but does He really have the time or patience to hear and respond to the common man? David inspires us to appreciate the loving, caring nature of our bond with God. We call out to God because we know in our deepest of thoughts that He will answer us. We further realize that His answer will not be a perfunctory one, a form letter response to our plea; we realize that the response will be based not only upon the words that we utter, but also on the depth of that need. Therefore, David writes, "Incline Your ear to me," an expression that evokes a desire on the part of the listener not to miss a word. God listens closely to our every sigh, as He counts our every tear.

Once we fathom the intimacy of our personal bond with God and the depth of concern and love that God has for His every creation, our reliance upon Him becomes complete and our faith restored.

Dedicated by
Seryl and Elliot Goldofsky

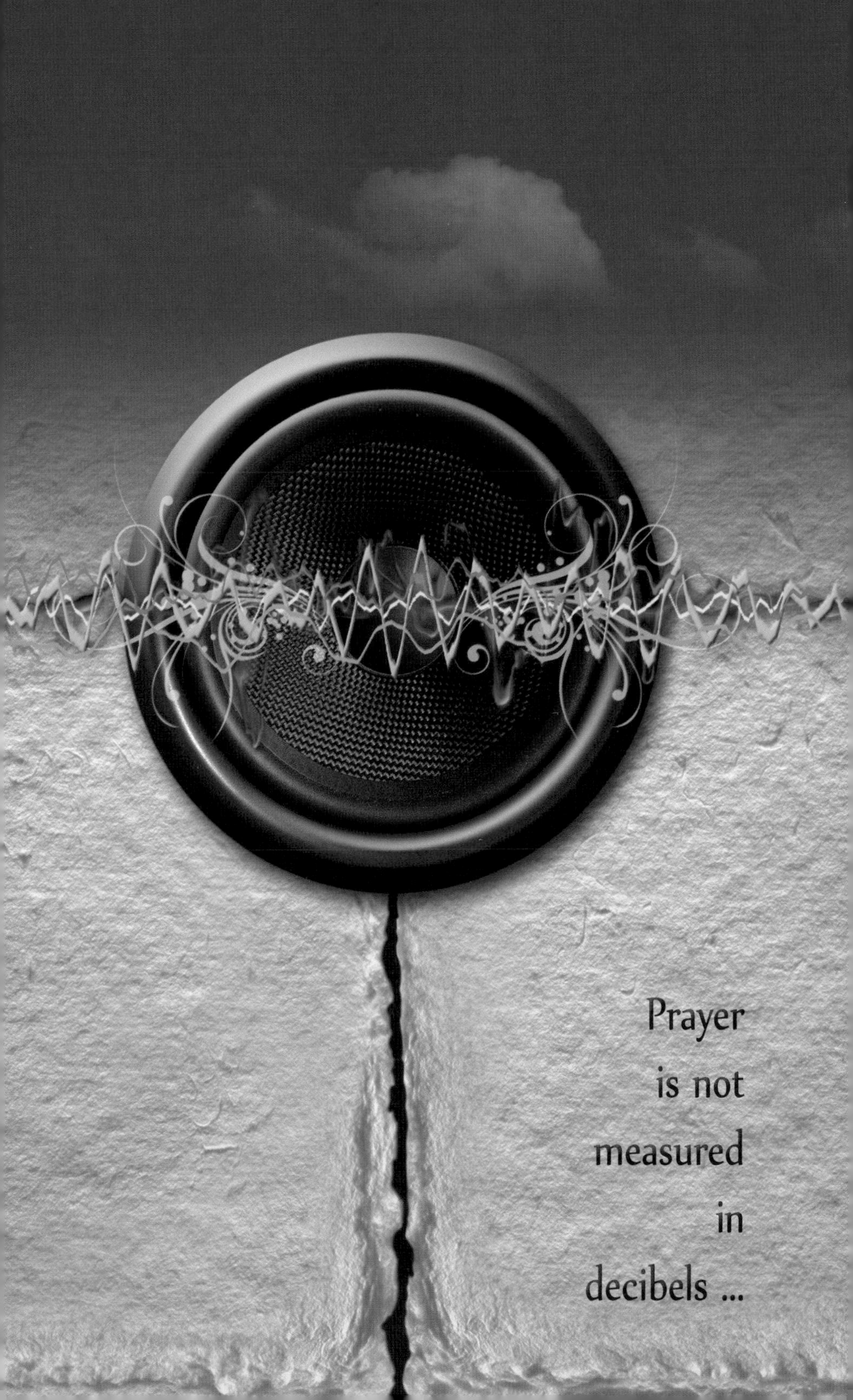
Prayer
is not
measured
in
decibels ...

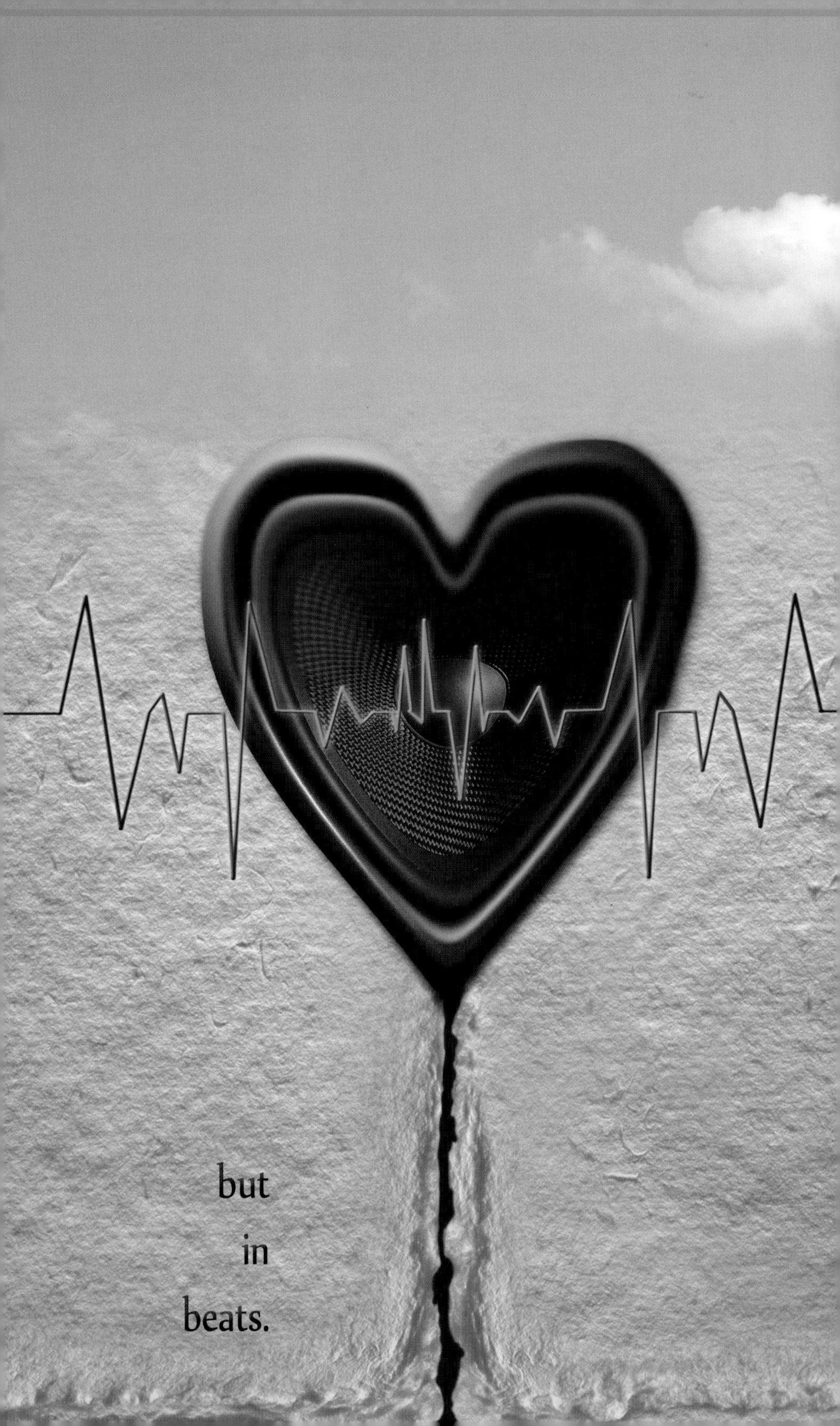
but
in
beats.

Reflections

Prayer is not measured in decibels . . .

but in beats.

-SL-

Eighteen

Psalm found on page 146

The road to hearing the divine response we seek is often a long and at times a tortuous path. While we would hope for an instant positive response to our every prayer and request, in this psalm, David, while celebrating God's salvation, charts a course of events that without an abiding faith would have led the weak of faith to falter along the way.

The ultimate victory over King Saul, which David records, was often met with temporary setbacks. In the psalm's flowing descriptive pattern, David describes the ebb and flow of God's sequence of events of which each one alone would lead one to despair. True, "God listened intently to my prayers and responded as He shook the mountains and the world trembled," but that event resulted in the creation of an all-consuming fire. The fiery smoke led to a blanket of darkness followed by hailstorms and flaming coal, arrows, and, ultimately, redemption.

At each interval, although God responded, it would have seemed to the nonbeliever that David's plight was worsened by the response. God's response of thundering mountaintops forces David to deal with uncontrollable fire and smoke. In contemporary terms, we may be in the midst of a medical protocol that will ultimately cure us, but in the process of healing we will experience added pain and suffering. Knowing from the start that setbacks are temporary while the cure is longstanding, would enable one to draw strength from within and battle on.

David calls upon us to draw on that strength and remain engaged in dialogue with God even as it may seem that events are unraveling around us. Through it all, God remains my strength as I take refuge, "my Shield, my Horn of Salvation, and my Stronghold."

Dedicated in honor of our treasured parents, in memory of our beloved mother, and in honor of our amazing children.
Tamar and Hillel Bryk

If we maintain our inner spark in spite of the scorching heat ...

we will
reach the
salvation
we so
desperately
seek.

Reflections

If we maintain our inner spark
in spite of the scorching heat . . .
we will reach the salvation we so desperately seek.
-SL-

Twenty

Psalm found on page 150

This chapter, often offered in times of crisis and concern, is filled with meaningful messages that can inspire our moments of prayer.

As Rashi explains, David expresses the belief that his power of prayer created the platform, the launching pad, as it were, for God to perform miracles in battle. "*Ki t'shuasam hee tshuasi*" — their redemption is in fact mine. Although David prompts God to help him prevail in battle, he does not expect to be victorious while sitting with his hands folded. Prayer alone is not a substitute for battle. Instead, the faith of the believer, as expressed through his prayer, provides the merit through which God provides salvation. As he prays, the man of faith fully accepts that the struggles of life must be confronted conventionally. Wars must be fought; doctors must be consulted and their orders followed. We must toil for our sustenance and our daily gift of life. David prays for the salvation of his troops even as he leads them into battle.

In this psalm, David invokes the name of Jacob (*Elokei Yaacov* — the God of Jacob) to the exclusion of Abraham and Isaac. Jacob prayed, explains the Malbim, outside the land of Israel, far from the security of the sanctity of place. David reminds us that prayer can be invoked from anywhere in the world and that God responds just as He does when man brings his offerings in the Temple in Jerusalem.

That is why this *tfila* is offered in times of crisis. We invoke David's power of prayer to create a new reality. We offer our prayer from anywhere in the world, confident that God will hear us and respond as if we were in His Temple. We erect a Temple in our hearts and in it we offer our fervent prayers.

Dedicated in memory of our parents
Dr. & Mrs. Stanley & Clara Evans שמואל פנחס בן צבי הלוי ז״ל חיה איטא בת הרב משה ע״ה

The long
exile has
turned
our hearts
to stone ...

fortunately, the
stone is that of
the Holy Temple,
and its capacity
to repair the tear
remains unaltered.

Reflections

The long exile has turned our hearts to stone . . .
fortunately, the stone is that of the Holy Temple,
and its capacity to repair the tear remains unaltered.
- SL -

Twenty Two

Psalm found on page 152

Man is created in the image of God, and we are often exhorted to reflect that image within the context of our daily lives. In so doing, our accomplishments reflect positively upon the image of God. A simple act of kindness unfolds into an opportunity for man to display the God-given qualities of compassion, goodness and sensitivity. Observers of these kind acts cannot help but extol the deity that designed man. When, on the other hand, our actions fall short of Godlike reflections, we bring potential desecration to the name of God and His dictates of life.

As we beseech God in prayer, we remain cognizant of the image that we reflect; and we often address our requests to Him based upon our being His representative in this world. Apparent in the many entreaties that David offers in prayer, is the sense that when salvation occurs to God's devoted people, it brings merit to God Himself. When a person becomes a star of industry, the world immediately wants to know who were the driving forces in that person's life.

David expresses to God that when He saves the weak, the downtrodden, and those in need — and He does so in a miraculous fashion — the entire world will take notice and heed His words. They will observe the devotion of His people, the nation's appreciation of His kindness, and God's benevolence towards those who reflect His image. "The humble will eat and be satisfied, those who seek God will praise Him — your hearts will live forever. All the nations of the world will turn back to God; all the families of nations will bow before You."

This message gives strength and encouragement to those in need of God's miracle. We plead with God to save us not for our sake and merit alone, but for the glory and honor that such a miracle may have upon a world in search of faith.

Dedicated in memory of Abraham and Yetta Schulman ע״ה
The Schulman family

The rising
moon does
little to
light up
the dark
night ...

rather, it
is the light
it reflects
which
reminds
us that the
sun will yet
rise.

Reflections

The rising moon does little to light up the dark night . . .
rather, it is the light it reflects which reminds us
that the sun will yet rise.
- SL -

Twenty Three

Psalm found on page 154

We instinctively feel comforted by God's embrace in times of joy, much as we feel a sense of divine rejection in moments of anguish and crisis. The cry of "Where is God?" looms over the individuals who are experiencing God's offensive when His ways differ from their desire, just as "Praise God!" is the public cry at His miraculous moments of salvation. The imbalance of these expressions can best be observed in the different rooms of a hospital. In one room there are tears of joy and thanksgiving upon the birth of a healthy child where family and friends gather in "praise" of God for His gift of life. In the very next room a baby is born with multiple disabilities, and the reaction is cries of "Where is He?"

David reminds us in this passage that both crisis and joy are derived from the same source and are, in fact, two sides of the same coin. The God that heals is the God that pains; each action, though seemingly in contradistinction to the other, emanates from the same "coin" of God's tangled involvement in man's daily life.

"Your rod and Your staff, they comfort me." In David's allegorical description of God as the shepherd and man as His sheep, the rod represents the crack of the stick on the hide of the wayward sheep, while the staff represents the protective arm distancing predators from assaulting His sheep. The painful rod and the loving staff "comfort me"; I am comforted by the realization that the crack of the stick is as protective of me and my needs as the embrace of the staff. I don't see its protective value, but, as David suggests, neither does the sheep.

The stinging pain of anguish must always be tempered by the appreciation of God's involvement throughout.

Dedicated by
Rena and Alan Schnall & Family

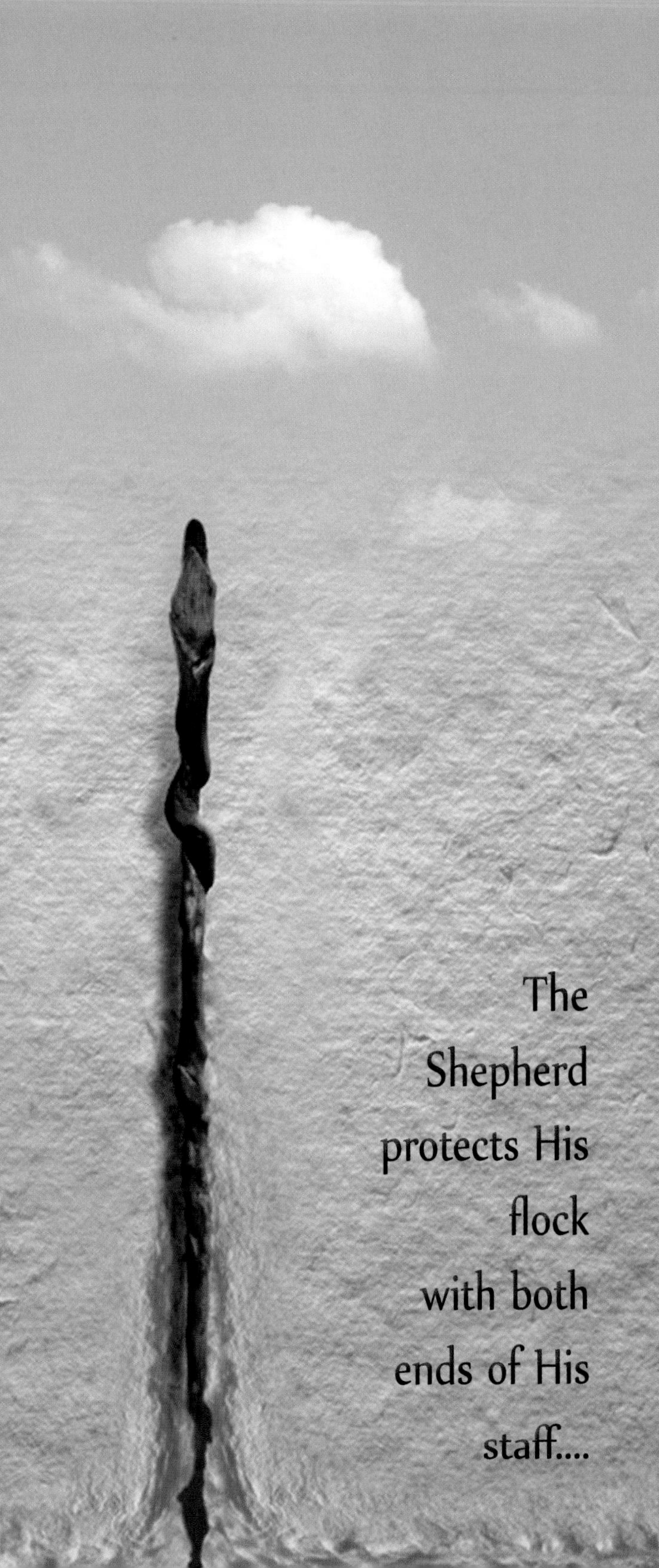
The
Shepherd
protects His
flock
with both
ends of His
staff....

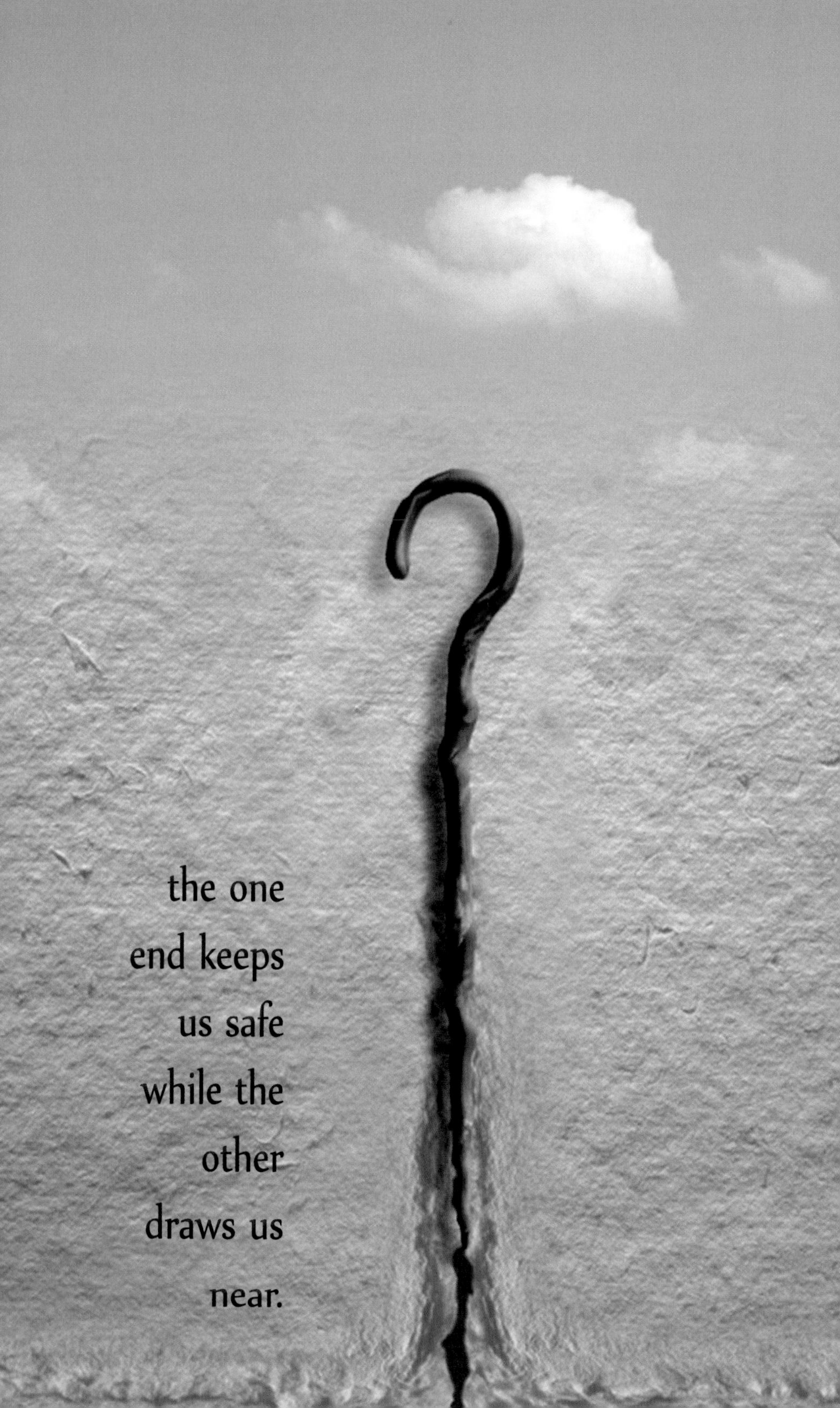
the one
end keeps
us safe
while the
other
draws us
near.

Reflections

The Shepherd protects His flock with both ends of His staff . . .
the one end keeps us safe while the other draws us near.
-SL-

Twenty Eight

Psalm found on page 154

In our moments of crisis, as we turn to God in prayer, we invoke Him with a full array of expressions of devotion and faith. We underscore our trust in His ways and the absolute rule over His dominion. David reminds us in this psalm that while prayer is critical, we need additional assistance from God to help us operate our daily lives in a Godly fashion.

"Do not be deaf to me; for should You be silent to me, I would be comparable to those who descend to the grave." This is not only a prayer to invoke God's compassion in crisis, but also more poignantly, a moment to implore God to assist man in living a life of devotion. David realizes that when the moment of need is upon us, we seek the solace of God. When the moment passes, we often revert back to a routine of life that is devoid of the passionate devotion that hallmarked our lives during the times of strain.

David turns to God for assistance, not in overcoming the obstacle of the moment, but more importantly, in safeguarding him from the pitfalls of the luring challenges of daily life that threaten to undermine the special relationship developed with God in times of prayer. It is David's request that He continue to stimulate that special bond by minimizing the travails of daily life and the challenges that often accompany its pursuit.

One manner in which to sustain the bond is to reaffirm the special relationship that God maintains with His people. "Save Your nation and bless Your inheritance; tend them and elevate them forever." We are not merely His nation. We are, in purpose and in mission, part of God's legacy. With that reality comes not only added responsibility, but also the faith that our bond is eternal.

Dedicated in memory of Stanley M. Klein ז״ל
Lost tragically on Swissair Flight 111

Our
efforts to
make it
past life's
hurdles ...

must also
break us free
from life's
monotonous
spin.

Reflections

Our efforts to make it past life's hurdles . . .
must also break us free from life's monotonous spin.
-SL-

Thirty

Psalm found on page 156

We are often urged to look at moments of grief and anguish as opportunities for not only reflection and prayer, but also as a time for reassessment. As we move along the expected path of life, we tend to travel the route on automatic pilot. We go through the motions of assessing our ways, but in reality, for the most part, until the extraordinary occurs, the path we travel is more often than not the path we traveled on all preceding days. When crisis strikes, yesterday's priority takes a back seat to a new order of need.

In this praising psalm, David introduces into his plea the sense that he has grown from his travails, and therefore, God need not delay his salvation any longer. He explains to God that in his present state, he realizes that God redeemed him from his many challenges and therefore merits the effusive expressions of praise that abound throughout the psalm. He compellingly adds, "What gain is there in my death, in my descent to the pit? Will the dust acknowledge You?" David evokes the vision of our day of death, a time when honest appraisals will prevail. At that time, we will praise every action that God performed, and the very action that caused our present pain will be retrospectively appreciated through the prism of a clearer perspective.

David therefore suggests that if the purpose of anguish is to reflect and ultimately to praise God in return for His actions, God need not seek man's demise, for the dead cannot offer the praise of the living. Instead, we present ourselves to God as one who thankfully acknowledges all of God's ways, as we implore Him to allow us to survive to continue to praise Him in act and in deed.

Dedicated by
Danny and Blimy Lemberg

More travelers have lost their way due to boredom ...

than due
to a poor
sense of
direction.

Reflections

More travelers have lost their way due to boredom ...
than due to a poor sense of direction.
-SL-

Thirty One

Psalm found on page 156

How does one begin a conversation with God? God knows our every action and foible, and appears as an imposing force difficult to face. How can we beseech Him for mercy, when there are clearly events in our lives that cause us to stand ashamed before Him? David appreciates this dilemma and addresses it directly and forthrightly in this psalm.

"In You, God, I have taken refuge, let me not be ashamed ever; in Your righteousness liberate me." David faces the challenge of speaking to God in shame, by including a liability as part of the request for salvation. David implores God to observe that we feel a sense of shame even as we urge Him to overlook it. David reminds God of His righteousness, compassion, and probative qualities that "have seen my affliction; You have taken note of the troubles of my soul." God not only sees the results of one's actions as they surface as one's "affliction", but knows the essence of the challenge, as He has probed "the troubles of my soul." Appreciating the profound depth of God's scrutiny can help liberate man from the chains of shame that may frustrate his opportunity to communicate with the Almighty. God has lived our troubles and has felt the depth of our challenges. He has full understanding of who we are as individuals and why we do what we do. With such intimate knowledge comes an openness that leaves room for error and repair.

Times of crisis and times of joy are moments of personal expression. David reminds us that during these moments, no matter what has preceded them, as we turn to the One Who knows us best, there will be a responsive ear to deeply felt expressions of the heart.

Dedicated in memory of
Milton Shedlin ז״ל

The surest
sign of
a bright
future...

is the
sight of
one's own
shadow.

Reflections

The surest sign of a bright future . . .

is the sight of one's own shadow.

-SL-

Thirty Two

Psalm found on page 158

Everything in life occurs for a reason. Although events may at times take on the appearance of mere happenstance, there is a divine plan of reason. One of man's challenges is to search for an element of that reason, even while mired in a world of confusion. True, many events that occur in our lives are beyond our scope of comprehension. These are most often unfathomable times of grief, both personal and communal, during which we spend all our days exploring the possible reasons for why we may have failed to divine His ways. In this context, however, David reminds us that there is a pattern of reward and punishment in life in a world that needs to be appreciated and understood.

"Be not like a horse, like a mule, uncomprehending, with muzzle and bridle to restrain when it is adorned, so that it not approach you." When tragedy befalls us, David urges us not to withdraw, not to remain passive, muzzled, bridled, and restrained, and not to fail to explore the reasons for the grief or the benefit of the temporal pain. We must use our gifts of intellect to search for meaning and purpose in tragedy. While we may not be able to comprehend the reasons behind the occurrence of tragic events, our probing mind will often find that kernel of purpose and benefit.

"For this let every devout one pray to You at a time when misfortune falls; only that the flooding, mighty waters not overtake him." If anguish must come, we pray to God that He offer it in "waves", not in "flooding mighty waters". We ask that He give us moments of respite in order to recharge our strength to battle the next challenge. Without the moments of calm between the storms, we must face the prospect of living through grief without moments of tranquility that enable us to explore its meaning and value.

Dedicated in memory of our dear parents
Herman & Esther Segal and Erich & Anna Weinberger

The roar of
the mighty
wave is not
meant to
deafen, but
to draw
attention ...

as is the
quiet of the
receding
wave not
meant to
lull, but to
offer a brief
respite.

Reflections

The roar of the mighty wave is not meant to deafen, but to draw attention ...

as is the quiet of the receding wave not meant to lull,
but to offer a brief respite.

-SL-

Thirty Three

Psalm found on page 160

We often wonder, what are the guiding principles that God employs in His decision-making process? Are these indications of what He can do – or better yet, what He will do? The clearer our understanding of His operating principles, the easier it is for man to follow those guidelines. At the same time, if the established guidelines are strictly enforced and we fail to live up to God's material life, we face moments of crisis in fearful despair rather than in hope. How will God respond to me when I have at times failed to respond to Him?

In this psalm, David explores the duality of approach. "God looks down from Heaven and sees all mankind. From His place of dwelling He oversees all inhabitants of the Earth." There is the universal operating principle that guides "all of mankind". Days and nights, the seasons of the year and the changes of weather, are all systems that are maintained equally by God for His people in the celestial realm of His creation. Nature remains a consistent operating principle. There is, however, a second system in place. "He oversees all the dwellers of the Earth." It is not the creative God that oversees all the dwellers, but rather the God of compassion and understanding. The God that appreciates that while Nature must be maintained equally for all, every one of His creations needs special care and understanding. The person seeking God in crisis is responded to differently than the person uttering the same words from a far less anxious place.

We are encouraged to implore the God of compassion to do the unexpected for us, just this one time. We ask that His understanding of our personal struggle drive Him to respond outside of the normal realm of Nature and heal our pain and renew our spirit.

Dedicated in memory of
Alex Lebovic ישעיה בן דב ז״ל

Long-
distance
binoculars
are for the
birds ...

precious
gems require
microscopic
care and
consideration.

Reflections

Long-distance binoculars are for the birds …
precious gems require microscopic care and consideration.
-SL-

Thirty Seven

Psalm found on page 162

In our battles of faith in times of challenge, we are, at times, confounded by the sights of scoundrels triumphing while the upstanding falter. We are not exploring why the righteous suffer while the undeserving are rewarded, a topic which deserves a far deeper analysis. There is, however, a prevailing by-product of the vexing reality; a by-product that David confronts and explores.

When faced with traumas of life, whether it be health, family or prosperity, we can easily question, "I try my best and all I have in life is despair – is it worth serving God if these are the results?" The dilemma is compounded when we view the undeserving succeeding beyond our dreams. In this passage, David urges us to appreciate more than what we see before our eyes. "Just a little longer, and then, wicked one, you will look carefully at his place and he will not be there." At the end of the day, whether in this world or in the world to come, the wicked will 'have no place'; therefore, David implies the place the wicked presently hold is of no real sustaining value; no matter how it glistens, its worth diminishes over time. Conversely, the perch of the faithful enhances in value now and forever. Perseverance in the face of challenge is not only an act of faith, but also a sound long-term investment in the pursuit of a purposeful meaningful life.

Devout passions are merely down payments for future sustenance. David knows that in times of crisis, we may want to walk away from the spiritual and good, throw our hands up and say it is just not working. He reminds us that in "just a little longer", we shall fully appreciate the broader achievements and success of good, and the vanishing success of evil.

Hold on and keep the faith.

Dedicated in memory of
Dr. Abraham and Ruth Naymark ע״ה

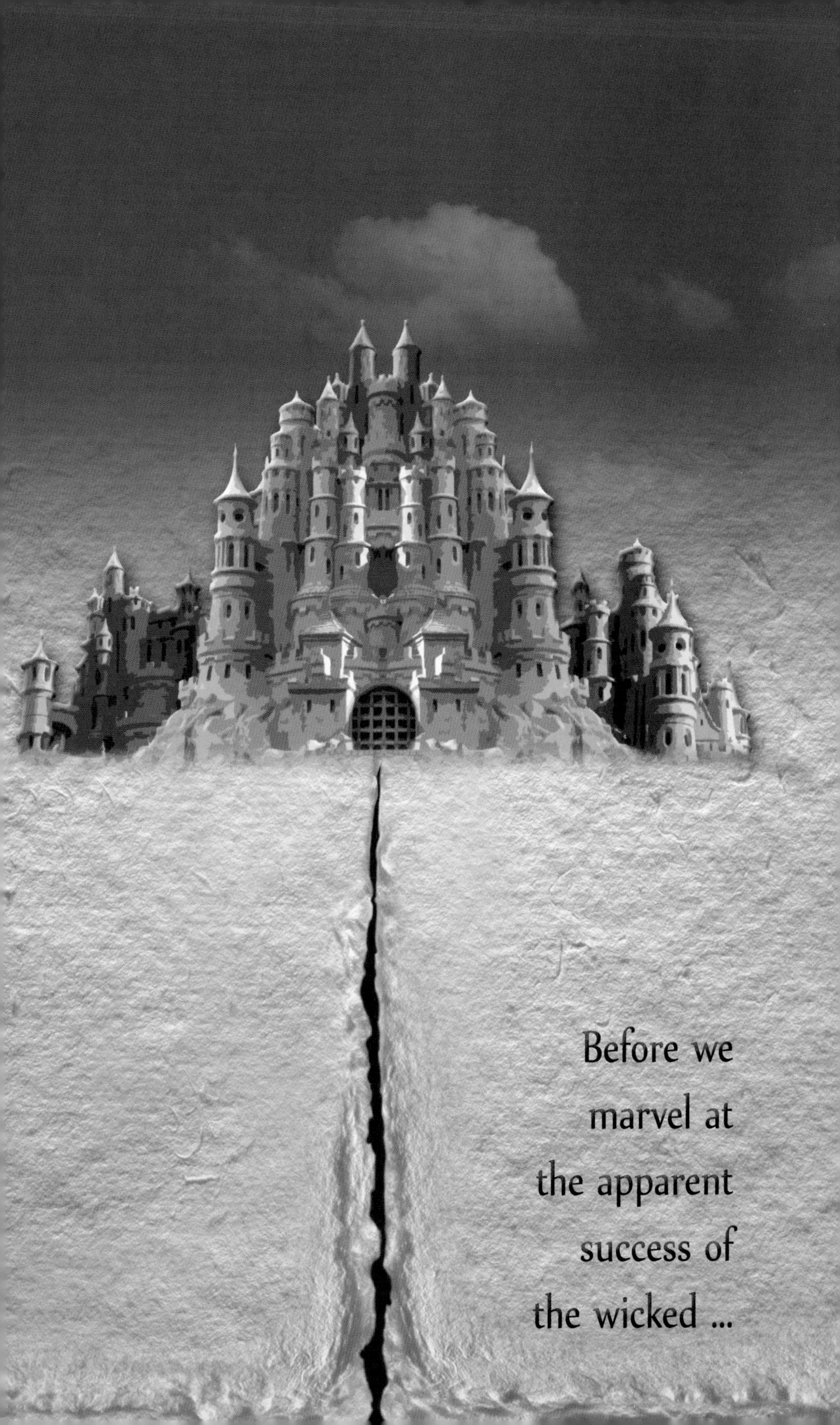
Before we
marvel at
the apparent
success of
the wicked ...

it would
serve us well
to wait for
the tide to
come in.

Reflections

Before we marvel at the apparent success of the wicked . . .
it would serve us well to wait for the tide to come in.

-SL-

Thirty Eight

Psalm found on page 164

Crisis and its accompanying pain is a lonely experience. At first, everyone is there to try to alleviate the pain; but over time, it becomes apparent that the crisis is a personal battle that will be won or lost from deep within.

The anguish of that inner struggle is expressed by David in terms that all who have gone through the pain of crisis recognize. In those moments of intense battle against despair, what is the ammunition at our disposal to confront that inner crisis? "My friends and companions, aloof from my affliction stand, and my close ones at a distance stand." We are told that these are the cherished friends that man possesses; his wealth, his family and friends, and the good deeds that he performs. Every act of kindness creates another friend, every expression of generosity another devoted soul mate. David tells us that in that inner struggle for mercy and healing before God, the money amassed will be spent and valueless, and family and friends will try to help but they too will prove to be helpless. What will remain at my side however, will be "my close ones at a distance stand," my acts of kindness stand with me in my struggle. I always perceived them to be at a distance from my fate in life, and yet, they will walk with me through my challenge and crisis.

It is for this reason that at times of challenge, we rededicate ourselves not only to fervent prayer before God, but to further acts of kindness and charity. The merit of those deeds remains at our side throughout the ordeals of life.

Dedicated in memory of
Joseph Diamond יוסף ב״ר יעקב צבי ז״ל

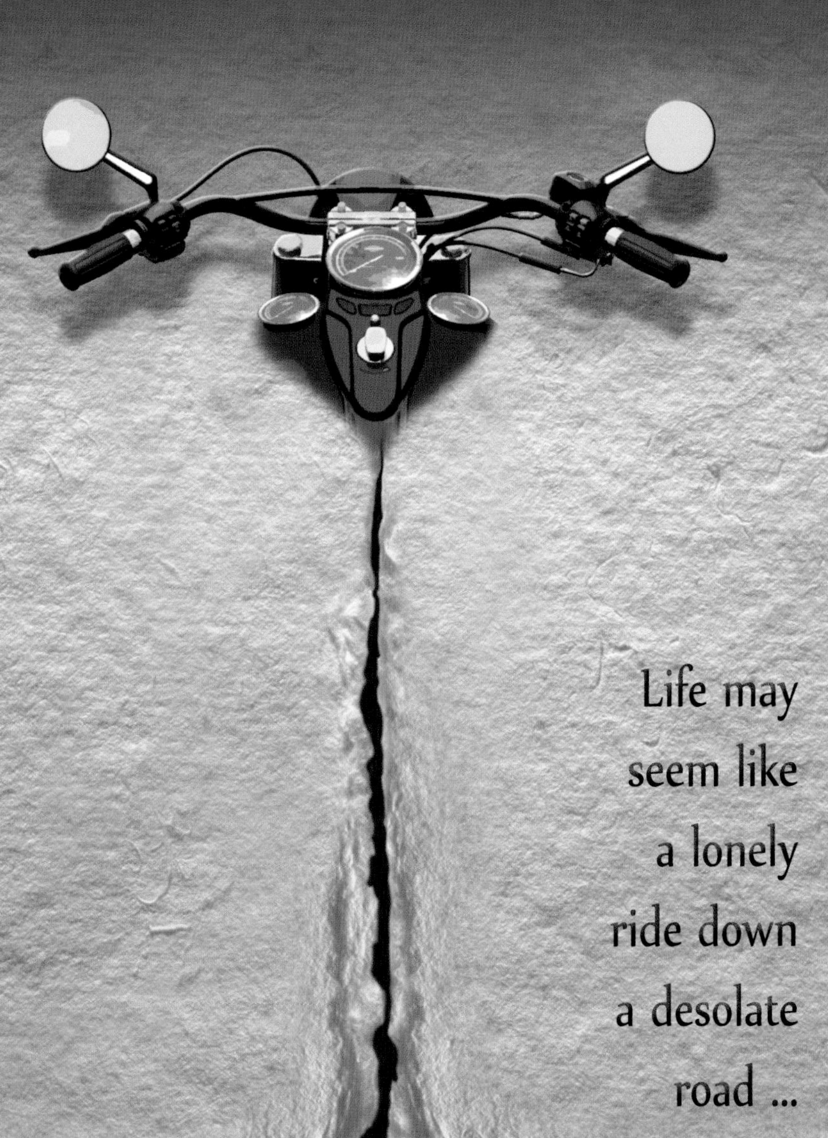

Life may
seem like
a lonely
ride down
a desolate
road ...

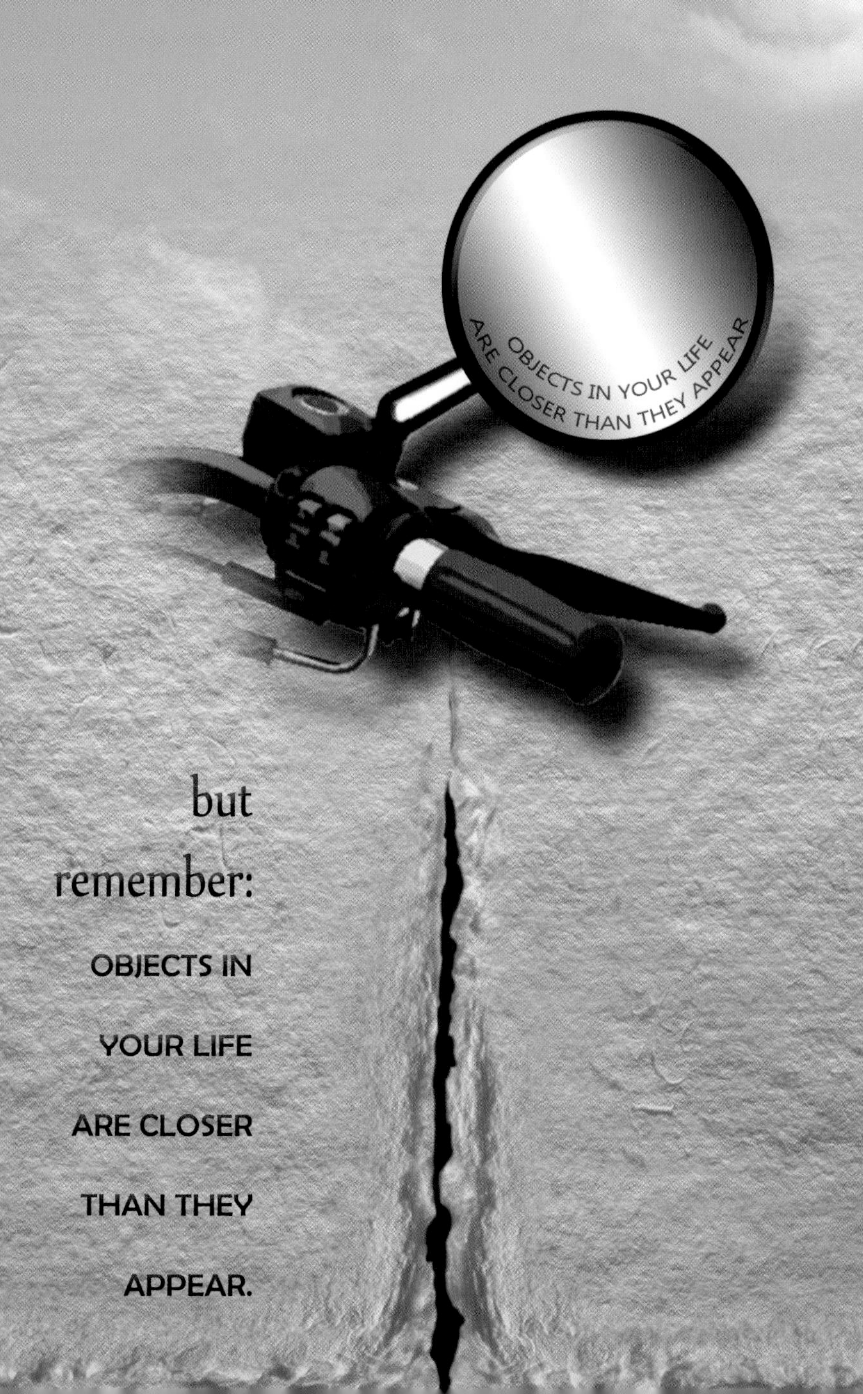
OBJECTS IN YOUR LIFE
ARE CLOSER THAN THEY APPEAR

but
remember:

OBJECTS IN YOUR LIFE ARE CLOSER THAN THEY APPEAR.

Reflections

Life may seem like a lonely ride down a desolate road . . .

but remember: OBJECTS IN YOUR LIFE ARE CLOSER THAN THEY APPEAR.

-SL-

Thirty Nine

Psalm found on page 166

In God's tapestry called creation, every thread, from the heavens and earth to the creatures beneath the sea, has its unique purpose. To be created means to serve a purpose in creation. Man, formed last in the cycle of creation, is charged with leading that mission of purposefulness in the world. Within a few mere moments of creation, Adam failed. With the ability of thought and speech, man was expected to achieve more in life than just live life – he was empowered to build a world and maintain it. He was encouraged to use his creativity and depth of knowledge to make a difference in the world. Illness and challenge can, at times, divert us from our mission.

This psalm describes the devastation that goes far deeper than the physical anguish of illness, worry, and struggle: "Remove from me Your plague; from the attack of Your hand I am devastated." David bemoans that he no longer can find purpose in his life; his soul cannot function, his creative gifts are dulled, his sense of Divine is lost. He is devastated! While the "plague" is a physical manifestation of illness or crisis, the devastation is the loss of the qualities that distinguished man in creation.

When reciting this psalm, we therefore join David in crying out to God; as we appreciate the depth of devastation, we feel unable to fulfill our mission in life. We pray to God to release us from our "plague" and restore our inner sense of mission.

Dedicated in memory of
Jack Greenblum ז״ל and Zev & Lisa Schmutter ז״ל

Creativity
is not
using the
light we
are given ...

it is
lighting
that
which we
are left
with.

Reflections

Creativity is not using the light we are given ...
it is lighting that which we are left with.
-SL-

Forty Nine

Psalm found on page 166

Two dynamics work within man: the body and the soul. The challenge of life is to synthesize the two into a single functioning entity that purposefully serves God, as it interfaces with the trials and triumphs of life. Our days are spent searching for the appropriate responses in life; responses that nurture the soul while they strengthen the body. Unfortunately, all too often, the needs of the body and soul are in conflict, and how we resolve that conflict ultimately defines who we are as God's creations. The creation that seeks the temporal joy of the body at the expense of satisfying the soul, shall find little solace after the initial charge of pleasure. Times of challenge are inherently times to reflect on the success of our balancing of service to body and soul.

In this psalm, David offers sobering insights into the eternity of our deeds. We shall not live forever and the actions of our days become the legacy of our lives. "For upon his death he will not take anything, his splendor will not descend after him." It is indeed true that upon death, the soul departs without any worldly possessions. The homes we built are left for others to enjoy. The deals we struck are for the benefit of those remaining behind. Nothing of temporal value descends to the grave with the body. At the same time, however, the soul can depart brimming with possessions of meaning, significance and value. The kindnesses performed, the charity offered, the sensitivities expressed in life, all become part of the luggage that the soul carries through eternity. Accomplishments defined as the splendor of the body "will not descend after him"; those defined as the splendor of the soul escort the soul through eternity.

Times of crisis and times of joy are opportunities to categorize the accomplishments we carry through our lives, and to internalize which of them will live on with us throughout our journey in time.

Dedicated in memory of our beloved Grandparents
by Julia and Norman Bobrow

Life's
baggage
can
either be
a
burden ...

or a
stairway
to
heaven.

Reflections

Life's baggage can either be a burden …

or a stairway to heaven.

-SL-

Fifty Six

Psalm found on page 168

This psalm portrays the proverbial helpless "dove of silence", who is distant from his home and without his natural sense of comfort. David was absolutely helpless, and fleeing from his homeland in what was perhaps the ultimate degradation, was forced to turn to yesterday's enemies for their assistance in protecting him from the danger being posed by today's foes. After he had been granted initial refuge, these enemies reneged – "all the day they make my words sorrowful; about me all their thoughts are for evil"– and once again demanded his life. Surrounded on literally all sides, David, in the depths of his troubles, cried out to God for assistance: "Cast the peoples down in anger, O God!"

Although his ongoing calamities were incredibly painful and seemingly beyond human ability to withstand, this psalm's heading is 'for the conductor'; David, amazingly keeping his sense of focus even as he literally does not know whether he shall survive till tomorrow. He sees that a guiding hand is exactingly conducting all that is transpiring. He does not understand why he was meant to undergo these sufferings. He realizes, however, that they are not haphazard, but that "You Yourself have counted my wanderings."

These crises are all part of God's plan, and they would not last for a moment longer than God initially planned for them to be, in order to fulfill their intended purpose. "I know that all of the tears that I have shed during my countless moments of pain are not meaningless history, but that 'You place my tears in Your flask,' and they become indelibly inscribed within Your eternal record.'" The moment that this flask of tears has become full, there is an immediate shift from tear to repair. "My foes will retreat", instantly, for "this I know: that God is with me", and is the source of all that is taking place.

Dedicated for the continued Refuah of
Ruchama Sara Miryam bat Tamar

The
ripple
effect of
each and
every
tear ...

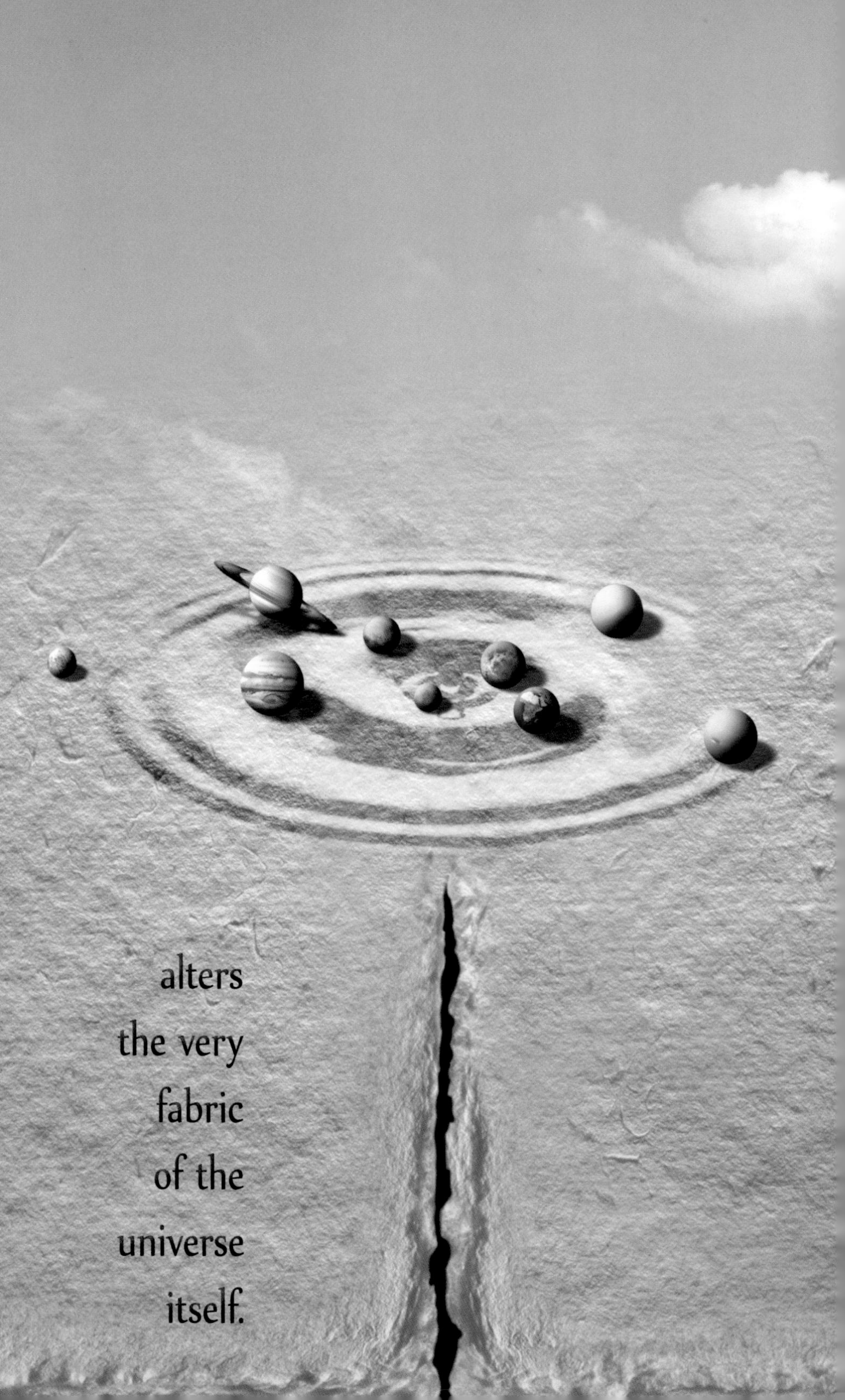

alters
the very
fabric
of the
universe
itself.

Reflections

The ripple effect of each and every tear . . .
alters the fabric of the universe itself.
-SL-

Eighty Six

Psalm found on page 170

This psalm, entitled 'A Prayer of David', offers us particular insight into the essence of our prayer relationship with God. David composed this psalm while fleeing his enemies, and repeatedly cried out to Hashem to save him from his mounting troubles. David implores God to "Incline Your ear, answer me ... save Your servant ... heed the sound of my supplications." Surprisingly, however, David's pleas during this time include other requests unrelated to his plea to survive. "All the nations that You have made will come and bow down before You, O Lord, and will give glory to Your Name," and "Teach me Your way, that I may travel in Your truth." Why was the request for enhanced spirituality included in David's moment of prayer for survival?

David is teaching us a lesson for all time — prayer to God is not only a means of alleviating the crisis that we face at the moment. It is, primarily, the opportunity to celebrate an enhanced and more robust relationship with God. Unfortunately, for most of us, prosperity and joy do not afford us those critical moments of introspection. We enjoy our good fortune while oftentimes failing to relate it to God's mastery over our world.

David encourages us to use this time of praying for need as a far-reaching opportunity to appreciate our inexorable bond with our Creator. It is often in those times of challenge that we rediscover the inspired soul we all possess so deep within.

Divine
demolition
comes ...

to reveal
rather
than to
wreck.

Reflections

Divine demolition comes . . .

to reveal rather than to wreck.

-SL-

Eighty Eight

Psalm found on page 170

The seemingly endless experiences of exile tests the mettle of even the greatest men of faith. The relentless battering of centuries of pogroms, expulsion and betrayal, by one nation after another, has battered the Jew, to the degree that David sees the Jew as "satiated with troubles." He cries out to God day and night as the only One Who can end this unceasing cycle of tragedies. David tearfully declares that "I was reckoned with those who descend to the pit, like a man without strength among the dead who are free, and am like the corpses lying in the grave, whom You remember no more, for they were cut off by Your hand. The overwhelming bitterness has consumed my life, the emptiness of which makes me feel as though I have already reached the grave, for You placed me in the lowest of pits, into utter darkness, into shadowy depths."

Are there any words of consolation to offer to someone so utterly disconnected from a life without suffering? The words of David both tear and repair. He refocuses his lens on the same picture with dramatically different results.

At the end of the day, what is the most dramatic distinction between those who languish in suffering and the "corpse laying the grave"? The only difference is that God has no ongoing nurturing and working relationship with the dead. No miracles are ever performed on their behalf. They in turn can no longer praise God nor appreciate His goodness. David suggests that although I may have been stripped of everything else, the fact that You, God, have left me with life — You continue to afford me opportunities for endless possibilities. You have not given up on me as I, in turn, turn in prayer to say, that I haven't given up on You. You continue to believe in me and value my achievements. You have faith in the living and we continue to demonstrate that faith in You.

Dedicated by
Sandy Nissel and Norman Horowitz & Rondi and Arthur Horowitz

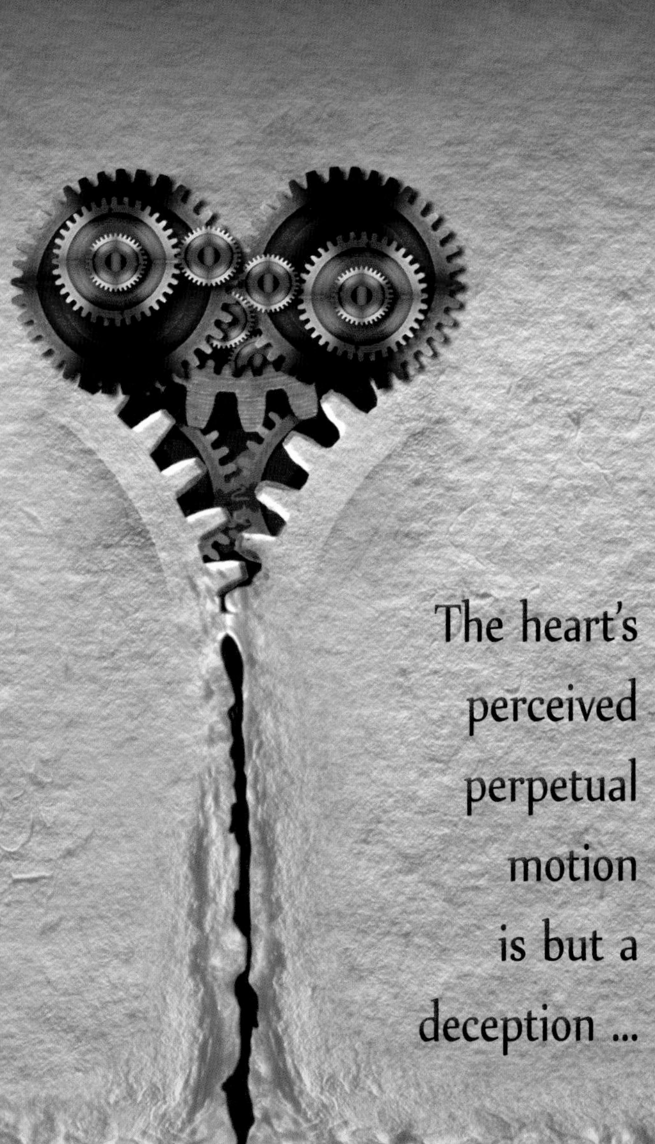
The heart's
perceived
perpetual
motion
is but a
deception ...

each beat
is a gift, a
responsibility,
an
opportunity.

Reflections

The heart's perceived perpetual motion is but a deception ...
each beat is a gift, a responsibility, an opportunity.
-SL-

Eighty Nine

Psalm found on page 172

The gifts of life, the ability to breathe, walk and talk, are all too often looked upon as rights rather than as gifts. It is no cause for particular celebration when those abilities which we feel are our entitlements, are provided for. Can we, when we are healthy, imagine a life that fails to follow the anticipated pattern — awakening from a restlful sleep, hearing the sounds of morning, feeling the sensation of the weather of every given season? In essence, while these are anticipated moments where the natural course of life rules, they are no less miraculous than the most outstanding miracle of God.

The first moment of a baby's life, the initial steps, and the first words uttered, are all moments of great anticipation and celebration. But as they recur every day and all day, appreciation of the nature of the miracle is further diluted to the point where the ongoing miracle is merely looked upon as life taking its natural course. Only when the extraordinary occurs or is needed to occur, do we once again turn to appreciate that which is often taken for granted.

David writes, "Your righteousness they are exalted," in order to instruct us that God's gifts of life and sustenance are not products of our merit, but of His righteousness; our prayers should be guided by that mindset. Rather than turn to God in prayer and proclaim, "God, You owe me - I deserve a miracle," we must recognize that we are recipients of God's gifts, not by virtue of our deeds, but rather because of His boundless love.

Dedicated in honor of our dear parents
Stanley and Raine Silverstein

What
we call
‘ordinary’,
is no less
than...

a
'miracle'
being
taken for
granted.

Reflections

What we call 'ordinary', is no less than …
a 'miracle' being taken for granted.
-SL-

Ninety

Psalm found on page 176

How can we cope with what is at times seemingly endless grief? What prayer can we offer to God that would adequately represent the depths of our pain and suffering, while at the same time signal to God that even at our lowest moments, we live with hope for a better tomorrow?

"Gladden us according to the days You have afflicted us. For years we saw evil." We ask God to renew our spirit and rebuild our strength, but we make the request even as we are driven by the anguish, pain and suffering that has been our destiny. I therefore turn to God and ask that He calculate, as only He can, the depth of my grief and "gladden my heart beyond that same measure." Who can fathom the pain felt with the loss of a child? Who can project the depth of grief of victims of terror? Who can feel the searing pain that explodes within, beyond the view of my fellow man? God sees, feels, and if He chooses, can compassionately respond.

We turn to God and offer a single prayer – Dear God, You know the depth of my despair; now is the time for equal levels of joy and ecstasy. You, dear God, know the anguish of my struggle. Now allow me to savor an equal portion of tranquility and joy. Gladden us according to the days You have afflicted us, the years that we faced evil. The pain will never leave us, but the abundance of joy that we pray for will ultimately refrain the grief as a prelude to ever-boundless joy.

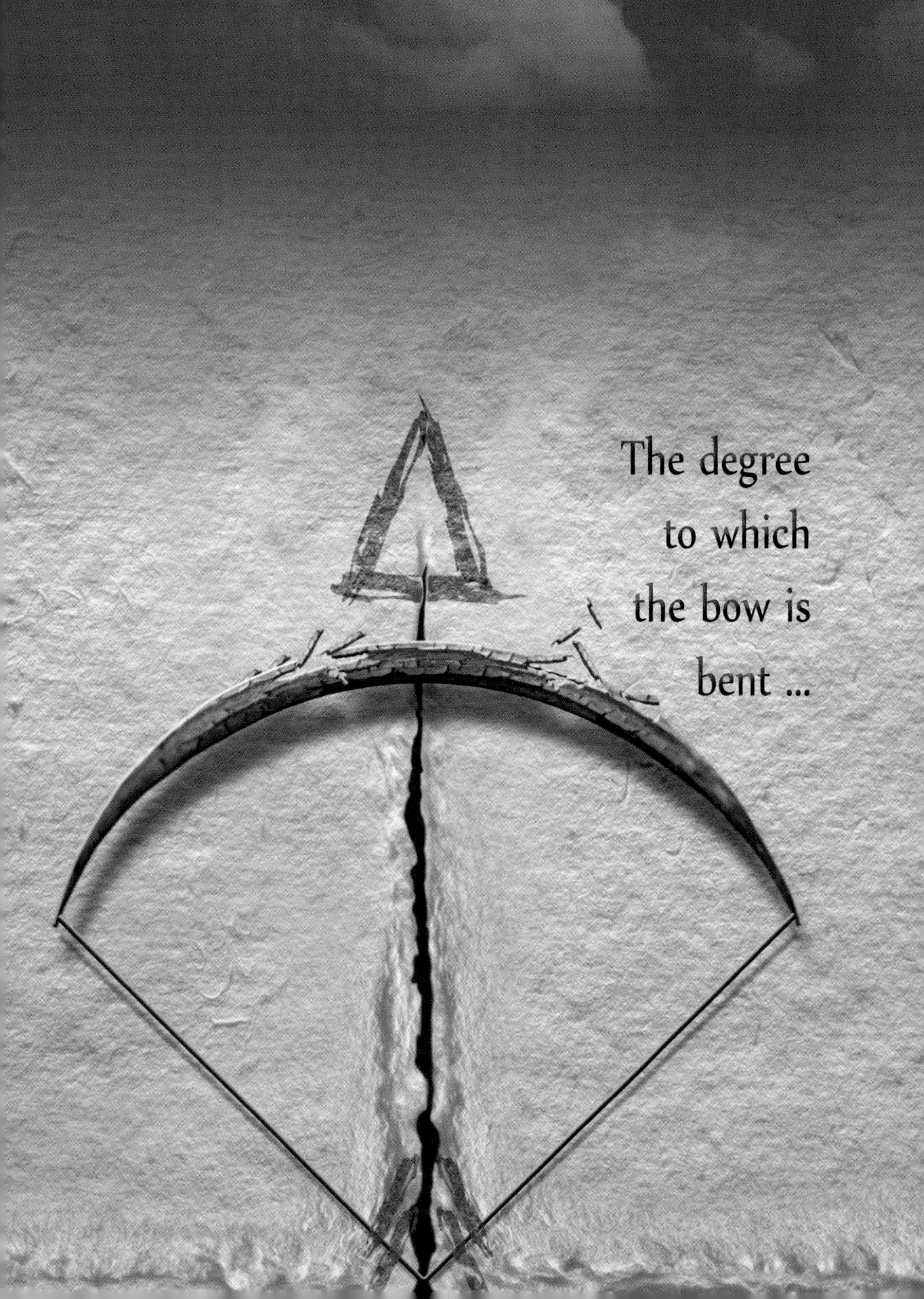
The degree
to which
the bow is
bent ...

determines
the height

to which the
arrow can
reach.

Reflections

The degree to which the bow is bent . . .
determines the height to which the arrow can reach.
-SL-

Ninety One

Psalm found on page 178

This psalm speaks of the beauty of a relationship with God, in which a person instinctively turns toward God's direction to guide his path in life. Aside from the sense of meaning that life now assumes on a daily basis, living in God's shadow further allows for His protective shade. Since his actions and activities are in line with nature, and not against it, there is simply no reason for harm to befall someone who lives by the Creator's guidance. David declares that "Having lived in this manner, I will state this truth openly, I will say of God, 'He is my refuge and my fortress' so that others also appreciate that 'He will deliver you from the ensnaring trap', and they too will ultimately live in a way in which they will benefit from God's protection."

A life with God brings along with that relationship a further benefit. The realization that while living in God's embrace does not always mean everything is going well— it does mean that it is following a divine course. Regrettably, I don't fully appreciate the course I've been tasked, but I have full faith that the end of this uncertain road will bring me to the destination tailored just for me. "Although a thousand may fall victim at your side and a myriad at your right hand, to you it shall not approach." Since you understand that to you these frightening dangers are simply irrelevant, you will simply not fear the terror of night, for you are living according to a larger and more perfect plan.

Dedicated in memory of
Tsivya bat Rivka ע״ה, David ben Rivka ז״ל & Yael bat Malka ע״ה

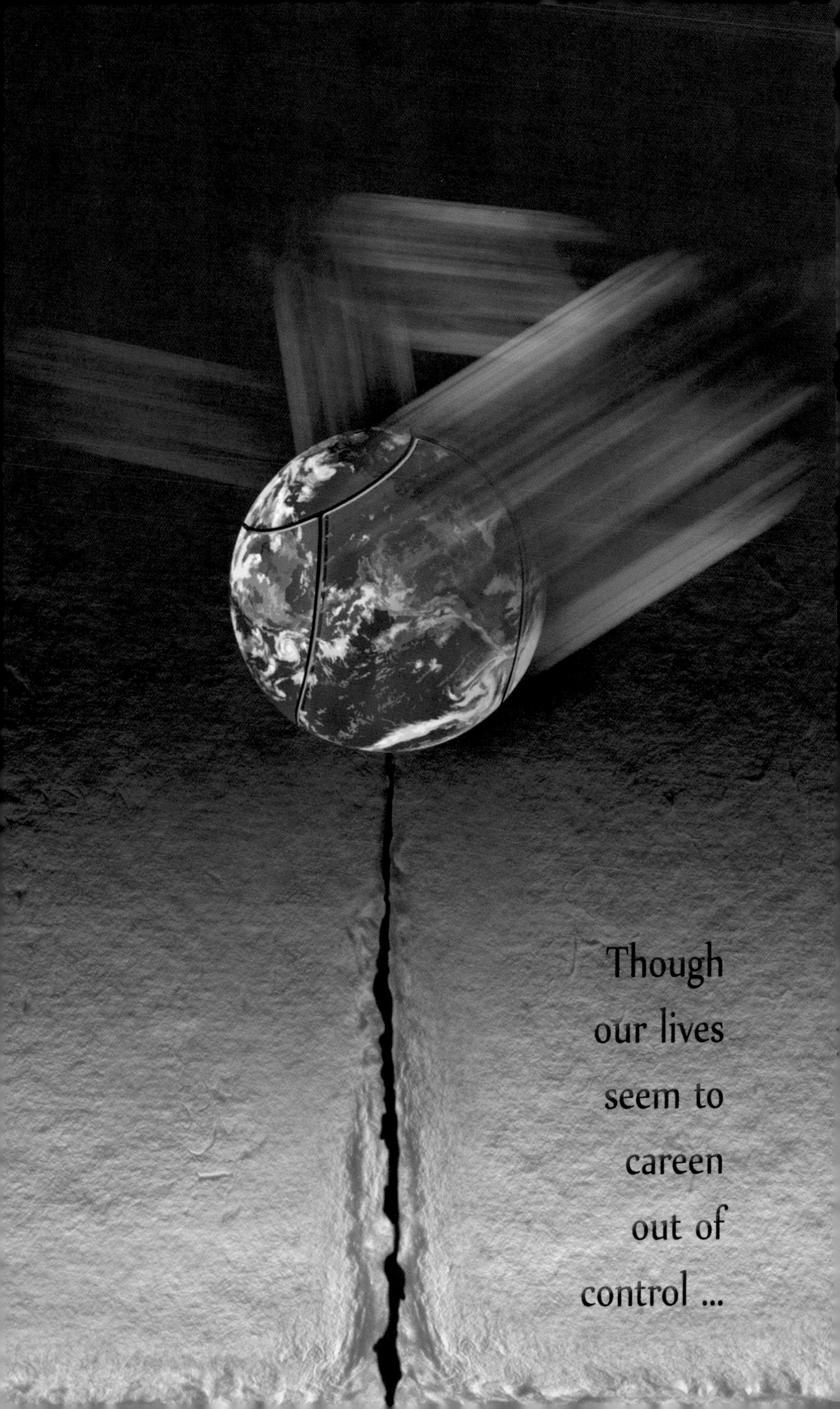

Though
our lives
seem to
careen
out of
control ...

they
remain
in tight
tether to
the One
up above.

Reflections

Though our lives seem to careen out of control . . .
they remain in tight tether to the One up above.
-SL-

One Hundred and Two

Psalm found on page 178

The prayer that is uttered by the person constantly afflicted by troubles is one long heartbreaking moan. God! Let my cry reach You! I have literally nothing left in life. Whatever I once had has totally disappeared, as if consumed by smoke, and my body is wracked with pain. My vitality has been totally sapped, like grass dried out by the hot sun. My loneliness is palpable, a sigh is constantly on my lips, and my enemies' ongoing reviling taunts are always in my ears.

What hope could this person possibly be given? In the world that surrounds him, indeed, nothing. All has been lost. His friends, possessions, and strength are long gone, never to return. The one source of comfort that this person has is that although nothing in the world that he sees around him is like the world that he once knew, he knows that one constant remains, God, Who he understands is eternal – "but You remain the same, and Your years will never end." Although he does not understand why God does what He does, he understands that life is not haphazard. The hardships that overwhelm me come only from "Your fury and Your wrath." We also understand that the God Who remains forever, will "in the final generation, hear the groaning of the prisoner, liberate those doomed to die."

In this psalm, David unfurls the blueprint of Jewish history, and in so doing, provides hope for us all. We frequently have no answers to life's ongoing difficulties. We are encouraged to realize that our suffering is not haphazard, but meticulously planned by the eternal God. Just as He is orchestrating our suffering, we know that He will soon bring an era of hope, when "You will arise and show Zion mercy, for there will come the time to favor her." Our role during our exiles and times of challenge is to maintain a love of God, and to use our internalized belief of redemption to navigate us through the challenges of the moment.

Dedicated in memory of
Septimus אליעזר צבי & Septimus חיה רחל & Hirth שמואל פישל ודבורה

The closer
to the
edge one
stands,
and the
greater
the
weight
one
bears ...

the higher
the
catapult
eventually
will be.

Reflections

The closer to the edge one stands, and the greater the weight one bears . . .

the higher the catapult eventually will be.

-SL-

One Hundred and Three

Psalm found on page 180

In this psalm, David repeatedly exclaims that his soul recognizes that God's kindness is ongoing and unique. Ongoing, for God provides for man throughout every stage of his life, in a way that only the soul – the part of man above and beyond his body – can appreciate. Unique in that, in contrast to the kindness that one man provides his friend, God's kindness elevates man to an altogether different level, to allow him to achieve what is impossible and even unthinkable in his present state. Instead of considering a person's actions and allowing this determination to shape His approach, God's transcending kindness is such that He views man from His heavenly perch far beyond the earth, and from this vantage, gives man the opportunity to do the same. Elevate yourselves heavenward.

This perspective is evident – on two levels. On a physical level, God delivers the fetus from the womb to experience a whole new world of living. He heals and will transform a deathly ill person into a perfectly healthy one, and in so doing, God allows us to achieve more than we could have imagined. On a more profound level, He allows us to survive beyond the transgressions that should condemn us. He distances us from the repercussion of our transgressions so that we may rise above them and ultimately realize our inner potential.

Although man is as frail and insignificant as a blade of grass easily blown away in a summer breeze, God nevertheless chooses to relate to us not only through our frailties but also through our potential; when we withstand our challenges, we and our progeny are secured the benefit of His kindness for eternity.

Dedicated in memory of
Renee' Gottlieb ע״ה & Joseph Harcsztark ז״ל

The
prevailing
winds, if
withstood...

will
eventually
carry us
aloft.

Reflections

The prevailing winds, if withstood . . .

will eventually carry us aloft.

-SL-

One Hundred and Sixteen

Psalm found on page 182

In the turmoil of challenge, we find no place of respite. We are caught in the torrents of uncertainty, fear, and anguish, often unable to find our bearings or roadmap to tranquility. From the depths of hopelessness, David defines our place of comfort, albeit not always our road to full repair and restoration.

"Return, my soul, to your rest; for God has been kind to you." David charges us to "take a deep breath", allow my soul to find its place of rest by appreciating that all that transpires is in God's hands; and in Him I bestow my full trust and faith. I may not be healed – I may not survive; but I will find a place of rest. I have within me the ability to find solace in the embrace of God, even in my moments of pain. When my path remains a trail of uncertainty, I feel comfort in empowering God to navigate my resolution. I maintain that I am at peace. I am in trouble, but I am no longer troubled. I have found my "place of rest" with God and in His trusted ways, my faith will evolve.

In the human cycle of life, the inconsistent patterns of joy and despair, health and illness, entering our world and departing it, allow for times of crisis and joy. Through it all, we can find our place of rest by encouraging our soul to seek the shelter of God in the acceptance of His plotted mission.

David probes this even deeper. He suggests we find our place of comfort with the knowledge that "God has been kind". What makes this all the more challenging is our difficulty in accepting the notion of God's kindness in a sea of turmoil. It requires reflection, introspection and faith. We are urged that in so doing, we will find the tranquility we seek.

Dedicated in honor of
Ludwig ז״ל & Lynne Engel

The
ripcord
can't halt
one's
descent ...

but it can
prevent
a crash
landing.

Reflections

The ripcord can't halt one's descent . . .

but it can prevent a crash landing.

-SL-

One Hundred and Eighteen

Psalm found on page 184

In times of crisis, there is always the cry of despair; but is there room for hope? How do we move beyond the present moment of challenge that we face, to a place of repair and relief? The ominous medical diagnosis, the impending financial disaster, and the despondent emotional state, create environments of spiritual torment, as well. How can I turn to God from my place of despair? In my feelings of God's abandonment, what prayer can I offer? What words do I want to offer?

David, in two passing phases, dispenses two kernels of suggested action at the dire moment of challenge. "Give thanks to God for He is good; for His kindness is enduring forever." His kindness is forever, unceasing, and, yes, even at times, beyond man's comprehension. The consistency of His kindness in sustaining us through the laws of nature, allowing us to live and function, to think and to act, all point to God's loving kindness, day in and day out — enduring forever. When we are faced with the unsettling event that undermines our appreciation of His goodness, we are urged to appreciate that God is pursuing an alternative trait in nurturing our sense of purposefulness in His world. Just as we appreciated His approach when times were good, David suggests we praise Him as an unending force of kindness, even when at a particular moment, He acts in ways beyond our comprehension.

When God challenges us with moments of torment and despair, David urges us to respond with faith and optimism. "I thank You, for You have answered me and You have been for me a salvation." We are encouraged to reframe our moments of crisis to the time of salvation. Move beyond the present, to a tomorrow of hope; live the present in the mindset of tomorrow.

Dedicated in loving memory of our parents
Rabbi Dr. Hillel & Gertrude Hochberg ע״ה, and Joseph & Ruth Ulevitch ע״ה

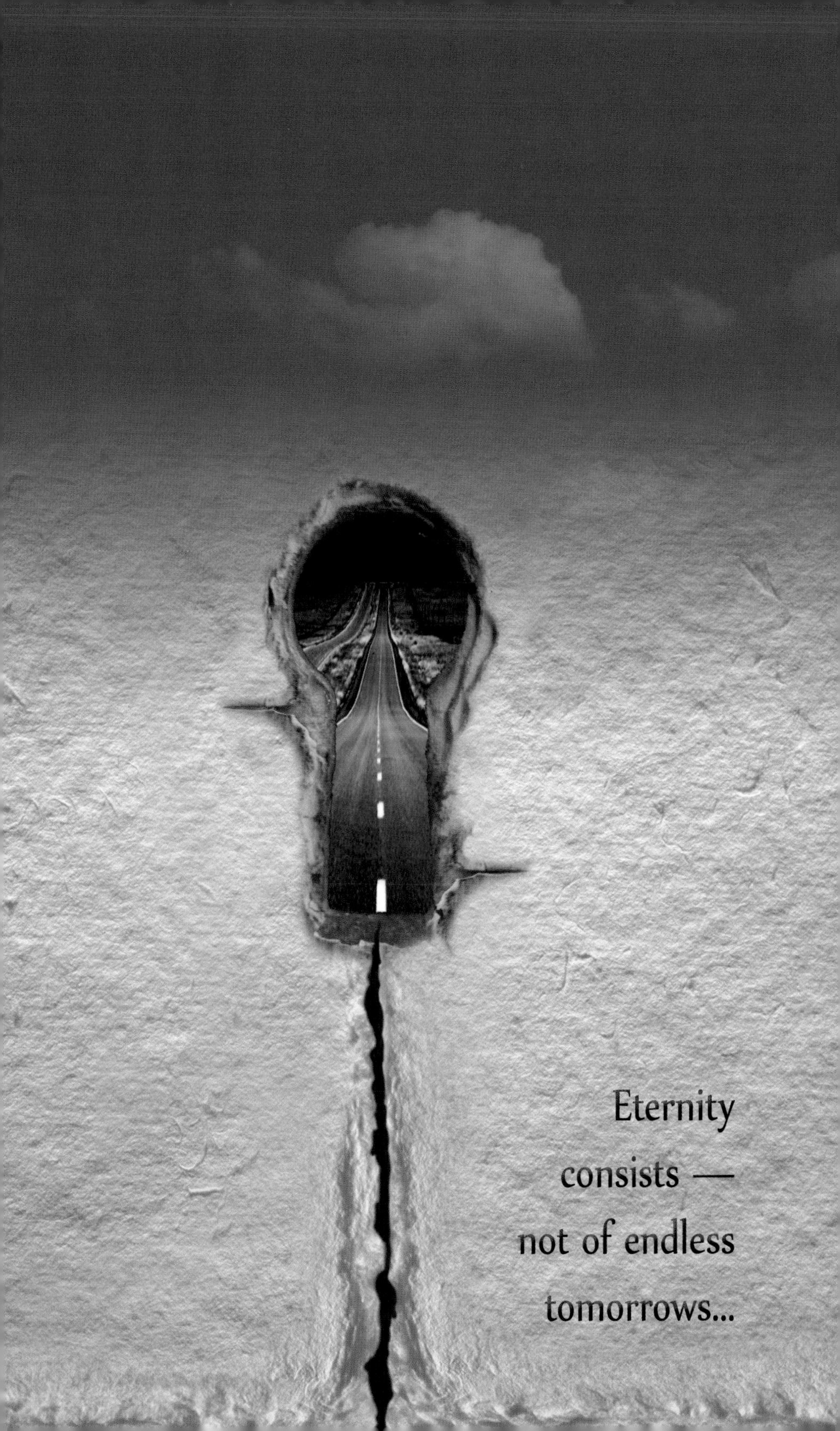
Eternity
consists —
not of endless
tomorrows...

but of a today
with endless
possibilities.

Reflections

Eternity consists – not of endless tomorrows . . .
but of a today with endless possibilities.
-SL-

One Hundred and Nineteen

Psalm found on page 186

We engage ourselves in those interests in life wherein we find our passion. A sports enthusiast will spend hours a day analyzing every nuance of the sport, all the while realizing that at the end of the day, his discussions have but little or no effect on the play unfolding on the field. And yet, we are driven to explore every statistic, every chart; the more we explore, the deeper the passion to explore even more. A similar exercise unfolds in every pursuit, from art appreciation to gardening; from business to fashion. The more we indulge ourselves in the pursuit, the deeper our passion and the greater our appreciation of that pursuit becomes. This even extends to faith in God and understanding His ways.

"Of Your precepts I speak and I look at Your paths." We ought not offer mere lip service expressing the greatness of our Creator. The effort demands heartfelt introspection that extends far deeper than mere bantering on faith. Seek out the message of God and His handiwork within the course of our daily lives. Find His glory in the tree that we plant, the air that we breathe, and the wind in our sails.

The more one speaks of God's gifts, strengths, dominance and omnipotence, the more one will discover and appreciate His ways. Then, and only then, *ashiva*– I will return to Him.

Dedicated in memory of
Barry David Reznik ע״ה & Beth Reznik Beller ע״ה

If absence
makes the
heart grow
fonder ...

fondness
makes the
soul draw
nearer.

Reflections

If absence makes the heart grow fonder…
fondness makes the soul draw nearer.
-SL-

One Hundred and Twenty One

Psalm found on page 194

Jacob, upon leaving the house of Isaac in mortal fear of his brother Esau, begins his march toward personal and national destiny. He will ultimately be the dominant patriarch, with the twelve tribes of Israel represented by his twelve sons.

But he has a long trek ahead — he will have to respond to the challenges of nemeses and yes, at times, even family. At the start of that journey, Jacob has a promise from God that He will never abandon him. With added bounce in his step, Jacob confronts his first challenge at the central watering well in proximity to the house of Lavan, where he will ultimately reside for a number of years.

In a telling verse at the well, Jacob asks the other water drawers — *mei-ayin atem*? "Where are you from? What brings us here together at this moment? Nothing in life is happenstance!" At which point Rachel appears, thereby leading Jacob on his path to greatness.

It began with a simple question of *mei-ayin atem*; or maybe not so simple. David, in this psalm, uses the same word to evoke the longing we have to find God even in the most unlikely places. *Mei-ayin yavo ezri* — "From where will my salvation come"? Jacob, perhaps, invokes this later call of David at his moment of challenge. He posits, "Is even this seemingly trivial moment, the moment of God's promise?" Jacob understands that at every moment and every encounter, God is his shadow and therefore ripe for His boundless kindness and love.

This stirring verse starting with a simple question of *mei-ayin*, unfolds as an inspiring chapter of comfort and faith. With the faith that God is always at my right side, we pray to Him to make this, the moment of tear to repair. We pray for our personal Rachel-Jacob moment to be now.

Dedicated by
Levi and Ahuva Meltzer

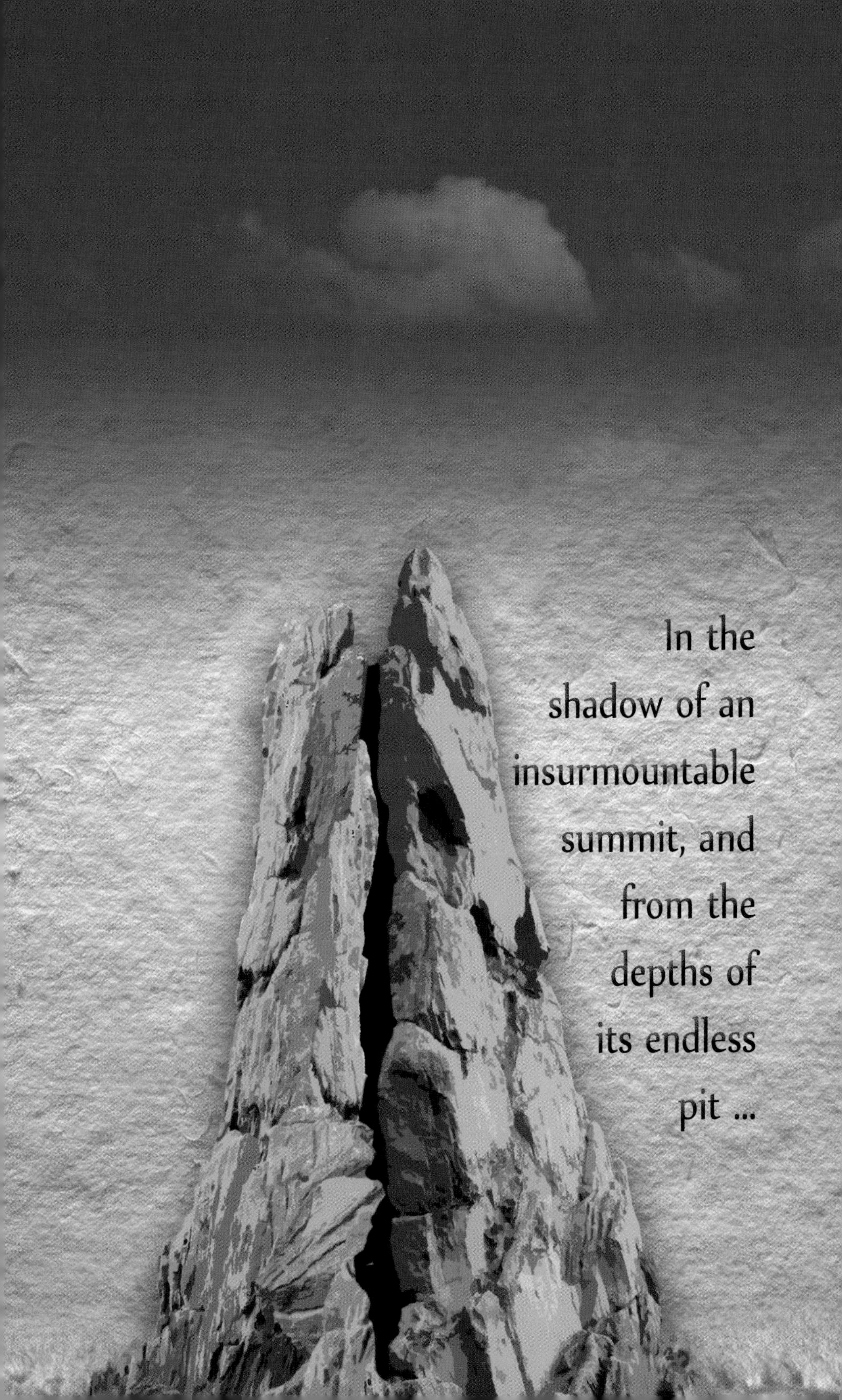
In the
shadow of an
insurmountable
summit, and
from the
depths of
its endless
pit ...

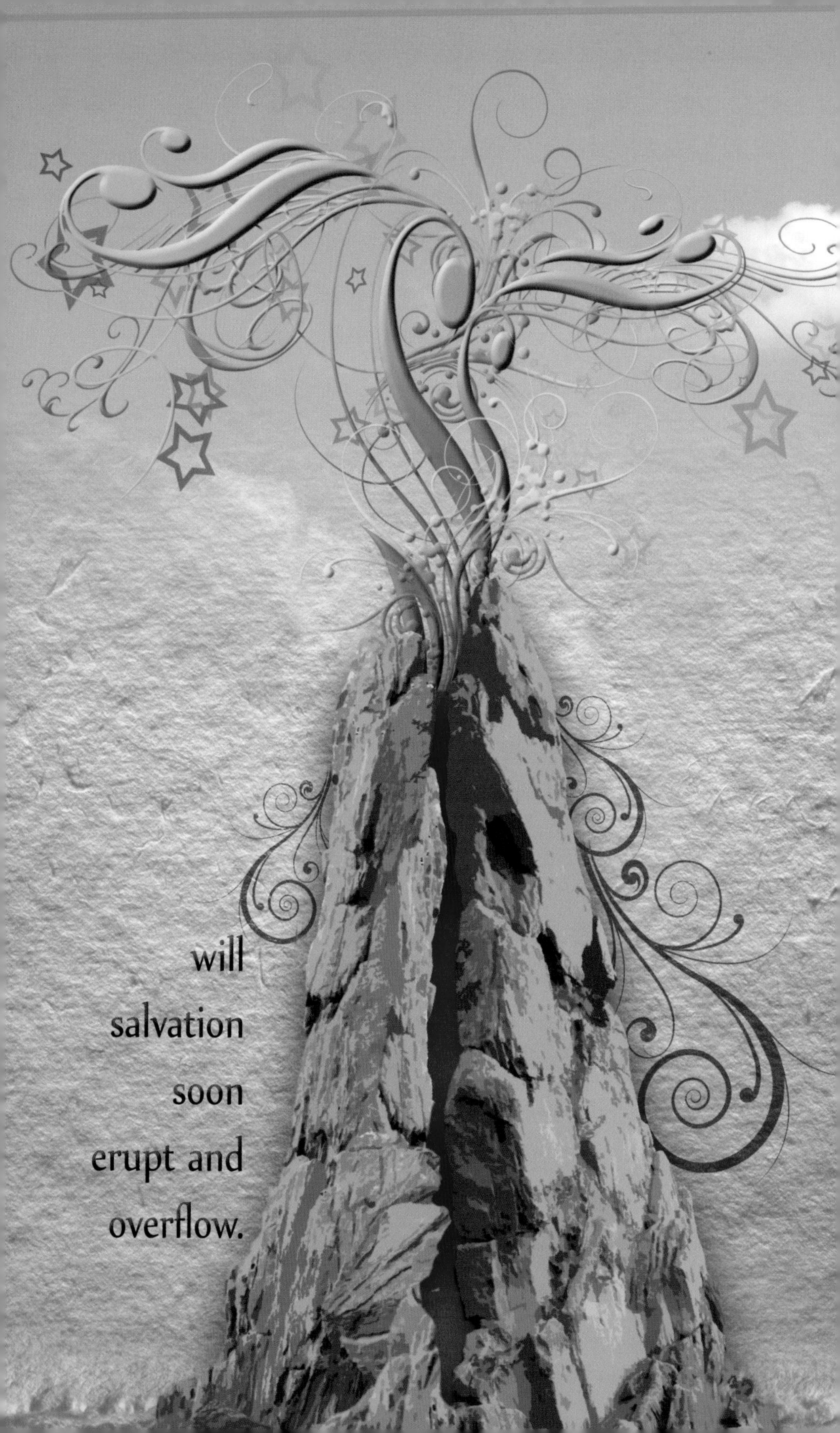

will
salvation
soon
erupt and
overflow.

Reflections

In the shadow of an insurmountable summit, and from the depths of its bottomless pit . . .

will salvation soon erupt and overflow.

-SL-

One Hundred and Forty Two

Psalm found on page 196

David recited this psalm while concealed in a cave, when he unexpectedly came upon the opportunity to kill King Saul, the very person who was actively seeking his death, and from whom he was hiding. When he chanced upon King Saul, David was struck by the overwhelming value of prayer, for, as the Midrash observes, there is no strength or wisdom of man that could have possibly engineered such an immediate end to his crisis.

David's insight into the power of prayer changed the outcome of the encounter. Upon further appreciating that God is the source of all that happens to man, David grabs the opportunity to beseech God for his salvation without having to kill his adversary. This prayer of David, therefore, is a remarkable expression of controlled emotions emanating from a deep recognition that if God intends to save him, David need not unnecessarily kill Saul.

"With my voice I cry out to Hashem' that I not fall into my adversary's hands, and 'with my voice I plead with Hashem' that he need not fall into mine. My only thoughts at this moment of prayer is that, 'I pour out my plaint before Him; I declare my distress before Him,' for this relationship with God will care for me in the best possible way. I plead with God for His creativity in resolving my challenge. Please God, 'release my soul from confinement'– from the limitations that we have created for ourselves in our approach to life – and allow me to fully 'acknowledge Your Name' as You masterfully arrange salvation in the way that You understand to be most fitting."

Truly inspired prayer invites man to appreciate God's dominance, thus allowing him to ask for the impossible. "Release my soul from confinement"; my prayers penetrate beyond known parameters. So too can God's response.

Dedicated in memory of Allen & Regina Hurwitz ע״ה
אליהו בן שלמה הלוי ע״ה & רבקה בת אברהם שלמה ע״ה

The
only thing
worse
than no
light at
the end
of the
tunnel...

is a rapidly
approaching
one.

Reflections

The only thing worse than no light at the end of the tunnel . . .
is a rapidly approaching one.
-SL-

One Hundred and Forty Eight

Psalm found on page 196

"I want to be left alone" is an often heard refrain in those episodes of life's daunting challenges. In solitude, we try to find hope and reason to events that appear on its surface as mere happenstance. David, in this psalm, redirects us to appraise life's events through God's mosaic of creation, of which we are but a small part, a speck in His universe of both time and space.

David urges us to reflect on all segments of creation: heaven and earth, the sun and the moon, the waters and its depths, fire, hail, wind, the mountain ranges and hills, meadows, trees, beasts, land animals, sea creatures, insects, birds, and, ultimately, the exalted creation of man. David's world view is that there is an inextricable link between all of God's creations, and in observing God's hand in every aspect of our environment, we are instinctively urged to sing, "Praise the Name of Hashem for His Name alone is exalted; His glory is above earth and heaven."

We must no longer look at any single event as separate and apart from God's master plan. Quite the contrary: the interlocking of all of God's creations encourages us to embrace the world and find solace, and appreciate that nothing is independent of God's tapestry of creation. And thus, we can never find solace in "being alone", but rather we must find it in the awareness and appreciation that we are part of God's master design.

When crisis hits, certainly the moment calls for inner reflection and searching, but at the same time, David guides us toward more fully internalizing that His handiwork spans our world. In so doing, we will find personal solace in praising God's benevolence even as we struggle with our challenge.

We feel the tear as we appreciate the repair.

Dedicated in honor of Bela and Emilio Goldstein & Edith and Eric Hanau
by their children, grandchildren and great-grandchildren

Those oddly
shaped
pieces, which
confound
and confuse...

will
eventually
come together
as the portrait
of our lives.

Reflections

Those oddly shaped pieces, which confound and confuse . . .
will eventually come together as the portrait of our lives.
-SL-

6

Reflections found on page 14

1. To the conductor with melodies on the *Sheminith*, a song of David. 2. O Lord, do not rebuke me in Your anger, and do not chastise me in Your wrath. 3. Be gracious to me, O Lord, because I languish; heal me, O Lord, because my bones are frightened. 4. And my soul is very frightened, and You, O Lord, how long? 5. Return, O Lord, rescue my soul; save me for the sake of Your loving- kindness. 6. For there is no memory of You in death; in the grave, who will thank You? 7. I am weary from my sighing; every night I sully my bed; I wet my couch with my tears. 8. My eye is dimmed from anger; it has aged because of all my adversaries. 9. Turn away from me, all you workers of iniquity, for the Lord has hearkened to the voice of my weeping. 10. The Lord has hearkened to my supplication; the Lord has accepted my prayer. 11. All my enemies shall be ashamed and very frightened; they shall return and be ashamed in a moment.

9

Reflections found on page 18

1. To the conductor, to brighten the youth, a song of David. 2. I will thank the Lord with all my heart; I will tell all Your wonders. 3. I will rejoice and exult with You; I will sing praises to Your most high name. 4. When my enemies draw backward, they stumble and are destroyed from before You. 5. For You have performed my judgment and my cause; You sat on the throne, O Judge of righteousness. 6. You rebuked nations, You destroyed a wicked man; You erased their name forever and ever. 7. The enemy has been destroyed; swords exist forever, and You have uprooted the cities-their remembrance is lost. 8. But the Lord shall sit forever; He has established His throne for judgment. 9. But He judges the world with righteousness, kingdoms with equity. 10. And the Lord shall be a fortress for the crushed, a fortress for times of distress. 11. And those who know Your name shall trust in You, for You have not forsaken those who seek You, O Lord. 12. Sing praises to the Lord, Who dwells in Zion; relate His deeds among the peoples. 13. For He Who avenges blood remembers them; He has not forgotten the cry of the humble. 14. Be gracious to me,

תהילים

ו

א לַמְנַצֵּחַ בִּנְגִינוֹת עַל־הַשְּׁמִינִית מִזְמוֹר לְדָוִד : ב יְהוָֹה
אַל־בְּאַפְּךָ תוֹכִיחֵנִי וְאַל־בַּחֲמָתְךָ תְיַסְּרֵנִי : ג חָנֵּנִי יְהוָֹה כִּי
אֻמְלַל אָנִי רְפָאֵנִי יְהוָֹה כִּי נִבְהֲלוּ עֲצָמָי : ד וְנַפְשִׁי נִבְהֲלָה
מְאֹד וְאַתְּ [וְאַתָּה] יְהוָֹה עַד־מָתָי : ה שׁוּבָה יְהוָֹה חַלְּצָה
נַפְשִׁי הוֹשִׁיעֵנִי לְמַעַן חַסְדֶּךָ : ו כִּי אֵין בַּמָּוֶת זִכְרֶךָ בִּשְׁאוֹל
מִי יוֹדֶה־לָּךְ : ז יָגַעְתִּי בְּאַנְחָתִי אַשְׂחֶה בְכָל־לַיְלָה מִטָּתִי
בְּדִמְעָתִי עַרְשִׂי אַמְסֶה : ח עָשְׁשָׁה מִכַּעַס עֵינִי עָתְקָה בְּכָל־
צוֹרְרָי : ט סוּרוּ מִמֶּנִּי כָּל־פֹּעֲלֵי אָוֶן כִּי־שָׁמַע יְהוָֹה קוֹל
בִּכְיִי : י שָׁמַע יְהוָֹה תְּחִנָּתִי יְהוָֹה תְּפִלָּתִי יִקָּח : יא יֵבֹשׁוּ
וְיִבָּהֲלוּ מְאֹד כָּל־אֹיְבָי יָשֻׁבוּ יֵבֹשׁוּ רָגַע :

ט

א לַמְנַצֵּחַ עַלְמוּת לַבֵּן מִזְמוֹר לְדָוִד : ב אוֹדֶה יְהוָֹה
בְּכָל־לִבִּי אֲסַפְּרָה כָּל־נִפְלְאוֹתֶיךָ : ג אֶשְׂמְחָה וְאֶעֶלְצָה בָךְ
אֲזַמְּרָה שִׁמְךָ עֶלְיוֹן : ד בְּשׁוּב־אוֹיְבַי אָחוֹר יִכָּשְׁלוּ וְיֹאבְדוּ
מִפָּנֶיךָ : ה כִּי־עָשִׂיתָ מִשְׁפָּטִי וְדִינִי יָשַׁבְתָּ לְכִסֵּא שׁוֹפֵט
צֶדֶק : ו גָּעַרְתָּ גוֹיִם אִבַּדְתָּ רָשָׁע שְׁמָם מָחִיתָ לְעוֹלָם וָעֶד :
ז הָאוֹיֵב | תַּמּוּ חֳרָבוֹת לָנֶצַח וְעָרִים נָתַשְׁתָּ אָבַד זִכְרָם
הֵמָּה : ח וַיהוָֹה לְעוֹלָם יֵשֵׁב כּוֹנֵן לַמִּשְׁפָּט כִּסְאוֹ : ט וְהוּא
יִשְׁפֹּט־תֵּבֵל בְּצֶדֶק יָדִין לְאֻמִּים בְּמֵישָׁרִים : י וִיהִי יְהוָֹה
מִשְׂגָּב לַדָּךְ מִשְׂגָּב לְעִתּוֹת בַּצָּרָה : יא וְיִבְטְחוּ בְךָ יוֹדְעֵי
שְׁמֶךָ כִּי לֹא־עָזַבְתָּ דֹרְשֶׁיךָ יְהוָֹה : יב זַמְּרוּ לַיהוָֹה יֹשֵׁב
צִיּוֹן הַגִּידוּ בָעַמִּים עֲלִילוֹתָיו : יג כִּי־דֹרֵשׁ דָּמִים אוֹתָם
זָכָר לֹא־שָׁכַח צַעֲקַת עֲנִיִּים [עֲנָוִים] : יד חָנְנֵנִי יְהוָֹה רְאֵה

O Lord, see my affliction from my enemies, You Who raise me up from the gates of death, 15. In order that I tell all Your praises; in the gates of the daughter of Zion I will rejoice in Your salvation. 16. Nations have sunk in the pit they have made; in this net that they have concealed, their foot has become trapped. 17. The Lord is known for the judgment that He performed; with the act of His hand, the wicked man stumbles. Let us meditate over this forever. 18. May the wicked return to the grave, all nations who forget God. 19. For the needy shall not be forgotten forever, neither shall the hope of the poor be lost to eternity. 20. Arise, O Lord; let man have no power. May the nations be judged for Your anger. 21. O Lord, place mastery over them; let the nations know that they forever are mortal man.

13

Reflections found on page 22

1. To the conductor, a song of David. 2. How long, O Lord? Will You forget me forever? How long will You hide Your face from me. 3. How long will I take counsel in my soul, having sorrow in my heart by day; how long will my enemy have the upper hand over me? 4. Look and answer me, O Lord my God; enlighten my eyes lest I sleep the sleep of death. 5. Lest my enemy say, "I have overwhelmed him"; my adversaries will rejoice when I totter. 6. But I trusted in Your loving-kindness, my heart will rejoice in Your salvation; I will sing to the Lord for He has bestowed [it] upon me.

16

Reflections found on page 26

1. A *Michtam* of David; O God, guard me for I have taken refuge in You. 2. You should say to the Lord, "You are my Master; my good is not incumbent upon You. 3. For the holy ones who are in the earth, and the mighty ones in whom is all my delight. 4. May the sorrows of those who hasten after another [deity] increase; I will not pour their libations of blood, nor will I take their names upon my lips. 5. The Lord is my allotted portion and my cup; You guide my destiny. 6. Portions have fallen to me in pleasant places; even the inheritance pleases me." 7. I will bless the Lord, Who counseled me; even at night my conscience instructs me. 8. I have placed the Lord before me constantly; because [He is] at my right hand, I will not falter. 9. Therefore, my heart rejoiced, and my soul was glad; even my flesh shall dwell in safety. 10. For You shall not forsake my soul to the

עָנְיִי מִשֹּׂנְאָי מְרוֹמְמִי מִשַּׁעֲרֵי מָוֶת : טו לְמַעַן אֲסַפְּרָה כָּל־
תְּהִלָּתֶיךָ בְּשַׁעֲרֵי בַת־צִיּוֹן אָגִילָה בִּישׁוּעָתֶךָ : טז טָבְעוּ גוֹיִם
בְּשַׁחַת עָשׂוּ בְּרֶשֶׁת־זוּ טָמָנוּ נִלְכְּדָה רַגְלָם : יז נוֹדַע ׀ יְהוָה
מִשְׁפָּט עָשָׂה בְּפֹעַל כַּפָּיו נוֹקֵשׁ רָשָׁע הִגָּיוֹן סֶלָה : יח יָשׁוּבוּ
רְשָׁעִים לִשְׁאוֹלָה כָּל־גּוֹיִם שְׁכֵחֵי אֱלֹהִים : יט כִּי לֹא לָנֶצַח
יִשָּׁכַח אֶבְיוֹן תִּקְוַת עֲנוִּים [עֲנִיִּים] תֹּאבַד לָעַד : כ קוּמָה
יְהוָה אַל־יָעֹז אֱנוֹשׁ יִשָּׁפְטוּ גוֹיִם עַל־פָּנֶיךָ : כא שִׁיתָה יְהוָה
׀ מוֹרָה לָהֶם יֵדְעוּ גוֹיִם אֱנוֹשׁ הֵמָּה סֶּלָה :

יג

א לַמְנַצֵּחַ מִזְמוֹר לְדָוִד : ב עַד־אָנָה יְהוָה תִּשְׁכָּחֵנִי
נֶצַח עַד־אָנָה ׀ תַּסְתִּיר אֶת־פָּנֶיךָ מִמֶּנִּי : ג עַד־אָנָה אָשִׁית
עֵצוֹת בְּנַפְשִׁי יָגוֹן בִּלְבָבִי יוֹמָם עַד־אָנָה ׀ יָרוּם אֹיְבִי עָלָי :
ד הַבִּיטָה עֲנֵנִי יְהוָה אֱלֹהָי הָאִירָה עֵינַי פֶּן־אִישַׁן הַמָּוֶת :
ה פֶּן־יֹאמַר אֹיְבִי יְכָלְתִּיו צָרַי יָגִילוּ כִּי אֶמּוֹט : ו וַאֲנִי ׀
בְּחַסְדְּךָ בָטַחְתִּי יָגֵל לִבִּי בִּישׁוּעָתֶךָ אָשִׁירָה לַיהוָה כִּי גָמַל
עָלָי :

טז

א מִכְתָּם לְדָוִד שָׁמְרֵנִי אֵל כִּי־חָסִיתִי בָךְ : ב
אָמַרְתְּ לַיהוָה אֲדֹנָי אָתָּה טוֹבָתִי בַּל־עָלֶיךָ : ג לִקְדוֹשִׁים
אֲשֶׁר־בָּאָרֶץ הֵמָּה וְאַדִּירֵי כָּל־חֶפְצִי־בָם : ד יִרְבּוּ עַצְּבוֹתָם
אַחֵר מָהָרוּ בַּל־אַסִּיךְ נִסְכֵּיהֶם מִדָּם וּבַל־אֶשָּׂא אֶת־שְׁמוֹתָם
עַל־שְׂפָתָי : ה יְהוָה מְנָת־חֶלְקִי וְכוֹסִי אַתָּה תּוֹמִיךְ גּוֹרָלִי :
ו חֲבָלִים נָפְלוּ־לִי בַּנְּעִמִים אַף־נַחֲלָת שָׁפְרָה עָלָי : ז אֲבָרֵךְ
אֶת־יְהוָה אֲשֶׁר יְעָצָנִי אַף־לֵילוֹת יִסְּרוּנִי כִלְיוֹתָי : ח שִׁוִּיתִי
יְהוָה לְנֶגְדִּי תָמִיד כִּי מִימִינִי בַּל־אֶמּוֹט : ט לָכֵן ׀ שָׂמַח לִבִּי
וַיָּגֶל כְּבוֹדִי אַף־בְּשָׂרִי יִשְׁכֹּן לָבֶטַח : י כִּי ׀ לֹא־תַעֲזֹב נַפְשִׁי

grave; You shall not allow Your pious one to see the pit. 11. You shall let me know the way of life, the fullness of joys in Your presence. There is pleasantness in Your right hand forever.

17

Reflections found on page 30

1. A prayer of David; Hearken, O Lord, to righteousness, listen to my cry, lend an ear to my prayer, [which is] without deceitful lips. 2. May my judgment come forth from before You; may Your eyes see [my] upright acts. 3. You have tried my heart; You have visited [upon me] at night. You have refined me and not found; If I think, let it not pass my mouth. 4. As for man's deeds, because of the word of Your lips, I kept [myself] from the ways of the profligate. 5. To support my feet in Your paths, lest my feet falter. 6. I called to You because You shall answer me, O God. Bend Your ear to me; hearken to my saying. 7. Distinguish Your kind acts to save, with Your right hand, those who take refuge [in You] from those who rise up [against them]. 8. Guard me as the apple of the eye; in the shadow of Your wings You shall hide me. 9. Because of the wicked who have robbed me; my mortal enemies who encompass me. 10. [With] their fat, they closed themselves up; their mouths spoke with haughtiness. 11. [By] our footsteps they surround us now, they set their eyes roaming over the land. 12. His likeness is like a lion, which yearns for prey, and as a young lion, which lurks in hidden places. 13. Arise, O Lord, confront him; bring him down to his knees; rescue my soul from the wicked, Your sword. 14. Of those who die by Your hand, O Lord, of those who die of old age, whose share is in life, and whose belly You will fill with Your hidden treasure, who have children in plenty and leave their abundance to their babes. 15. I will see Your face with righteousness; I will be satisfied with Your image upon the awakening.

18

Reflections found on page 34

1. For the conductor; of the servant of the Lord, of David, who spoke to the Lord the words of this song on the day that the Lord saved him from the hand of all his enemies and from the hand of Saul. 2. And he

לִשְׁאוֹל לֹא־תִתֵּן חֲסִידְךָ לִרְאוֹת שָׁחַת׃ יא תּוֹדִיעֵנִי אֹרַח
חַיִּים שֹׂבַע שְׂמָחוֹת אֶת־פָּנֶיךָ נְעִמוֹת בִּימִינְךָ נֶצַח׃

יז

א תְּפִלָּה לְדָוִד שִׁמְעָה יְהוָה | צֶדֶק הַקְשִׁיבָה רִנָּתִי
הַאֲזִינָה תְפִלָּתִי בְּלֹא שִׂפְתֵי מִרְמָה׃ ב מִלְּפָנֶיךָ מִשְׁפָּטִי
יֵצֵא עֵינֶיךָ תֶּחֱזֶינָה מֵישָׁרִים׃ ג בָּחַנְתָּ לִבִּי | פָּקַדְתָּ לַּיְלָה
צְרַפְתַּנִי בַל־תִּמְצָא זַמֹּתִי בַּל־יַעֲבָר־פִּי׃ ד לִפְעֻלּוֹת אָדָם
בִּדְבַר שְׂפָתֶיךָ אֲנִי שָׁמַרְתִּי אָרְחוֹת פָּרִיץ׃ ה תָּמֹךְ אֲשֻׁרַי
בְּמַעְגְּלוֹתֶיךָ בַּל־נָמוֹטּוּ פְעָמָי׃ ו אֲנִי קְרָאתִיךָ כִי־תַעֲנֵנִי אֵל
הַט־אָזְנְךָ לִי שְׁמַע אִמְרָתִי׃ ז הַפְלֵה חֲסָדֶיךָ מוֹשִׁיעַ חוֹסִים
מִמִּתְקוֹמְמִים בִּימִינֶךָ׃ ח שָׁמְרֵנִי כְּאִישׁוֹן בַּת־עָיִן בְּצֵל
כְּנָפֶיךָ תַּסְתִּירֵנִי׃ ט מִפְּנֵי רְשָׁעִים זוּ שַׁדּוּנִי אֹיְבַי בְּנֶפֶשׁ
יַקִּיפוּ עָלָי׃ י חֶלְבָּמוֹ סָּגְרוּ פִּימוֹ דִּבְּרוּ בְגֵאוּת׃ יא אַשֻּׁרֵינוּ
עַתָּה סְבָבוּנִי [סְבָבוּנוּ] עֵינֵיהֶם יָשִׁיתוּ לִנְטוֹת בָּאָרֶץ׃ יב
דִּמְיֹנוֹ כְּאַרְיֵה יִכְסוֹף לִטְרוֹף וְכִכְפִיר יֹשֵׁב בְּמִסְתָּרִים׃
יג קוּמָה יְהוָה קַדְּמָה פָנָיו הַכְרִיעֵהוּ פַּלְּטָה נַפְשִׁי מֵרָשָׁע
חַרְבֶּךָ׃ יד מִמְתִים יָדְךָ | יְהוָה מִמְתִים מֵחֶלֶד חֶלְקָם
בַּחַיִּים וּצְפִינְךָ [וּצְפוּנְךָ] תְּמַלֵּא בִטְנָם יִשְׂבְּעוּ בָנִים וְהִנִּיחוּ
יִתְרָם לְעוֹלְלֵיהֶם׃ טו אֲנִי בְּצֶדֶק אֶחֱזֶה פָנֶיךָ אֶשְׂבְּעָה
בְהָקִיץ תְּמוּנָתֶךָ׃

יח

א לַמְנַצֵּחַ | לְעֶבֶד יְהוָה לְדָוִד אֲשֶׁר דִּבֶּר | לַיהוָה
אֶת־דִּבְרֵי הַשִּׁירָה הַזֹּאת בְּיוֹם | הִצִּיל־יְהוָה אוֹתוֹ מִכַּף כָּל־
אֹיְבָיו וּמִיַּד שָׁאוּל׃ ב וַיֹּאמַר אֶרְחָמְךָ יְהוָה חִזְקִי׃ ג יְהוָה

said, "I love You, O Lord, my strength. 3. O Lord, my rock and my fortress and my rescuer; my God, my rock, I will take refuge in Him; my shield and the horn of my salvation, my refuge. 4. With praise I call to the Lord, and from my enemies I will be saved. 5. Bands of death have encompassed me, and streams of scoundrels would affright me. 6. Bands of the nether world have surrounded me; the snares of death confronted me. 7. When I am in distress, I call upon the Lord; yes, I cry out to my God; out of His temple He hears my voice, and my cry comes before Him in His ears. 8. The earth shook and quaked, the foundations of the mountains did tremble; and they were shaken when He was angered. 9. Smoke went up in His nostrils, and fire out of His mouth did devour; coals flamed forth from Him. 10. And He bent the heavens, and He came down, and thick darkness was under His feet. 11. And He rode on a cherub and did fly; He swooped on the wings of the wind. 12. He made darkness His hiding-place about Him as His booth; the darkness of waters, thick clouds of the skies. 13. From the brightness before Him, His thick cloud passed, hail and coals of fire. 14. The Lord thundered from Heaven; and the Most High gave forth His voice with hail and coals of fire. 15. And He sent out arrows and He scattered them; He shot lightning and He discomfited them. 16. And the depths of the water appeared; the foundations of the world were laid bare by Your rebuke, O Lord, by the blast of the breath of Your nostrils. 17. He sent forth from on high [and] He took me; He drew me out of many waters. 18. He delivered me from my mighty enemy, and from those that hated me, for they were too powerful for me. 19. They confronted me on the day of my calamity, but the Lord was a support to me. 20. And He brought me forth into a wide space; He delivered me because He took delight in me. 21. The Lord rewarded me according to my righteousness; according to the cleanness of my hands He recompensed me. 22. For I have kept the ways of the Lord and have not wickedly departed from [the commandments of] my God. 23. For all His ordinances were before me; and His statutes I will not remove from myself. 24. And I was single-hearted with Him, and I kept myself from my iniquity. 25. And the Lord has recompensed me according to my righteousness, according to the cleanness of my hands before His eyes. 26. With a kind one, You show Yourself kind, with a sincere man, You show Yourself sincere. 27. With a pure one, You show Yourself pure, but with a crooked one, You deal crookedly. 28. For You deliver a humble people, and You humble haughty eyes. 29. For You light my lamp; the Lord, my God, does light my darkness. 30. For by You I run upon a troop, and by my God I scale a wall. 31. [He is] the God Whose way is perfect; the word of the Lord is refined; He is a shield to all who trust in

סַלְעִי וּמְצוּדָתִי וּמְפַלְטִי אֵלִי צוּרִי אֶחֱסֶה־בּוֹ מָגִנִּי וְקֶרֶן
יִשְׁעִי מִשְׂגַּבִּי׃ ד מְהֻלָּל אֶקְרָא יְהֹוָה וּמִן־אֹיְבַי אִוָּשֵׁעַ׃ ה
אֲפָפוּנִי חֶבְלֵי־מָוֶת וְנַחֲלֵי בְלִיַּעַל יְבַעֲתוּנִי׃ ו חֶבְלֵי שְׁאוֹל
סְבָבוּנִי קִדְּמוּנִי מוֹקְשֵׁי מָוֶת׃ ז בַּצַּר־לִי | אֶקְרָא יְהֹוָה וְאֶל־
אֱלֹהַי אֲשַׁוֵּעַ יִשְׁמַע מֵהֵיכָלוֹ קוֹלִי וְשַׁוְעָתִי לְפָנָיו | תָּבוֹא
בְאָזְנָיו׃ ח וַתִּגְעַשׁ וַתִּרְעַשׁ | הָאָרֶץ וּמוֹסְדֵי הָרִים יִרְגָּזוּ
וַיִּתְגָּעֲשׁוּ כִּי חָרָה לוֹ׃ ט עָלָה עָשָׁן בְּאַפּוֹ וְאֵשׁ מִפִּיו תֹּאכֵל
גֶּחָלִים בָּעֲרוּ מִמֶּנּוּ׃ י וַיֵּט שָׁמַיִם וַיֵּרַד וַעֲרָפֶל תַּחַת רַגְלָיו׃
יא וַיִּרְכַּב עַל־כְּרוּב וַיָּעֹף וַיֵּדֶא עַל־כַּנְפֵי־רוּחַ׃ יב יָשֶׁת חֹשֶׁךְ
| סִתְרוֹ סְבִיבוֹתָיו סֻכָּתוֹ חֶשְׁכַת־מַיִם עָבֵי שְׁחָקִים׃ יג
מִנֹּגַהּ נֶגְדּוֹ עָבָיו עָבְרוּ בָּרָד וְגַחֲלֵי־אֵשׁ׃ יד וַיַּרְעֵם בַּשָּׁמַיִם
| יְהֹוָה וְעֶלְיוֹן יִתֵּן קֹלוֹ בָּרָד וְגַחֲלֵי־אֵשׁ׃ טו וַיִּשְׁלַח חִצָּיו
וַיְפִיצֵם וּבְרָקִים רָב וַיְהֻמֵּם׃ טז וַיֵּרָאוּ | אֲפִיקֵי מַיִם וַיִּגָּלוּ
מוֹסְדוֹת תֵּבֵל מִגַּעֲרָתְךָ יְהֹוָה מִנִּשְׁמַת רוּחַ אַפֶּךָ׃ יז יִשְׁלַח
מִמָּרוֹם יִקָּחֵנִי יַמְשֵׁנִי מִמַּיִם רַבִּים׃ יח יַצִּילֵנִי מֵאֹיְבִי עָז
וּמִשֹּׂנְאַי כִּי־אָמְצוּ מִמֶּנִּי׃ יט יְקַדְּמוּנִי בְיוֹם אֵידִי וַיְהִי
יְהֹוָה לְמִשְׁעָן לִי׃ כ וַיּוֹצִיאֵנִי לַמֶּרְחָב יְחַלְּצֵנִי כִּי חָפֵץ בִּי׃
כא יִגְמְלֵנִי יְהֹוָה כְּצִדְקִי כְּבֹר יָדַי יָשִׁיב לִי׃ כב כִּי־שָׁמַרְתִּי
דַּרְכֵי יְהֹוָה וְלֹא־רָשַׁעְתִּי מֵאֱלֹהָי׃ כג כִּי כָל־מִשְׁפָּטָיו לְנֶגְדִּי
וְחֻקֹּתָיו לֹא־אָסִיר מֶנִּי׃ כד וָאֱהִי תָמִים עִמּוֹ וָאֶשְׁתַּמֵּר
מֵעֲוֹנִי׃ כה וַיָּשֶׁב־יְהֹוָה לִי כְצִדְקִי כְּבֹר יָדַי לְנֶגֶד עֵינָיו׃
כו עִם־חָסִיד תִּתְחַסָּד עִם־גְּבַר תָּמִים תִּתַּמָּם׃ כז עִם־נָבָר
תִּתְבָּרָר וְעִם־עִקֵּשׁ תִּתְפַּתָּל׃ כח כִּי־אַתָּה עַם־עָנִי תוֹשִׁיעַ
וְעֵינַיִם רָמוֹת תַּשְׁפִּיל׃ כט כִּי־אַתָּה תָּאִיר נֵרִי יְהֹוָה אֱלֹהַי
יַגִּיהַּ חָשְׁכִּי׃ ל כִּי־בְךָ אָרֻץ גְּדוּד וּבֵאלֹהַי אֲדַלֶּג־שׁוּר׃ לא
הָאֵל תָּמִים דַּרְכּוֹ אִמְרַת יְהֹוָה צְרוּפָה מָגֵן הוּא לְכֹל |
הַחוֹסִים בּוֹ׃ לב כִּי מִי אֱלוֹהַּ מִבַּלְעֲדֵי יְהֹוָה וּמִי־צוּר זוּלָתִי
אֱלֹהֵינוּ׃ לג הָאֵל הַמְאַזְּרֵנִי חָיִל וַיִּתֵּן תָּמִים דַּרְכִּי׃ לד

Him. 32. For who is God save the Lord? And who is a Rock, save our God?
33. The God is He Who girds me with strength; and He makes my way
perfect. 34. He makes my feet like hinds, and sets me upon my high places.
35. He trains my hands for war so that a copper bow is bent by my arms.
36. You have given me the shield of Your salvation; Your right hand has
supported me, and You have treated me with great humility. 37. You have
enlarged my step[s] beneath me, and my ankles have not slipped. 38. I have
pursued my enemies and overtaken them, never turning back until they
were consumed. 39. I have crushed them so that they cannot rise; yea, they
are fallen under my feet. 40. For You have girded me with strength for the
battle; You have subdued under me those that rose up against me. 41. And
of my enemies, You have given me the back of their necks; those that hate
me, that I may cut them off. 42. They pray but no one saves them; [even]
to the Lord, but He answered them not. 43. Then I ground them as dust
before the wind; as the mud in the streets I did pour them. 44. You allowed
me to escape from the contenders of the people; You shall make me the
head over nations; may a people that I do not know serve me. 45. As soon
as they hear they shall obey me; foreigners shall lie to me. 46. Foreigners
shall wither, and they shall fear their imprisonments. 47. The Lord lives,
and blessed be my Rock, and exalted be the God of my salvation. 48. The
God Who grants me vengeance and destroys peoples instead of me. 49.
Who delivers me from my enemies; even above those that rise against me
You have lifted me; from the violent man You deliver me. 50. Therefore, I
will give thanks to You, O Lord, among the nations, and to Your name I
will sing praises. 51. He gives great salvations to His king, and He performs
kindness to His anointed; to David and to his seed forever.

20

Reflections found on page 38

1. For the conductor, a song of David. 2. May the Lord
answer you on a day of distress; may the name of the God of Jacob fortify
you. 3. May He send your aid from His sanctuary, and may He support
you from Zion. 4. May He remember all your meal offerings and may He
accept your fat burnt offerings forever. 5. May He give you as your heart
[desires], and may He fulfill all your counsel. 6. Let us sing praises for your
salvation, and let us assemble in the name of our God; may the Lord fulfill
all your requests. 7. Now I know that the Lord saved His anointed; He
answered him from His holy heavens; with the mighty acts of salvation
from His right hand. 8. These trust in chariots and these in horses, but we-

מְשַׁוֶּה רַגְלַי כָּאַיָּלוֹת וְעַל בָּמֹתַי יַעֲמִידֵנִי׃ לה מְלַמֵּד יָדַי
לַמִּלְחָמָה וְנִחֲתָה קֶשֶׁת־נְחוּשָׁה זְרוֹעֹתָי׃ לו וַתִּתֶּן־לִי מָגֵן
יִשְׁעֶךָ וִימִינְךָ תִסְעָדֵנִי וְעַנְוָתְךָ תַרְבֵּנִי׃ לז תַּרְחִיב צַעֲדִי
תַחְתָּי וְלֹא מָעֲדוּ קַרְסֻלָּי׃ לח אֶרְדּוֹף אוֹיְבַי וְאַשִּׂיגֵם וְלֹא־
אָשׁוּב עַד־כַּלּוֹתָם׃ לט אֶמְחָצֵם וְלֹא־יֻכְלוּ קוּם יִפְּלוּ תַּחַת
רַגְלָי׃ מ וַתְּאַזְּרֵנִי חַיִל לַמִּלְחָמָה תַּכְרִיעַ קָמַי תַּחְתָּי׃
מא וְאֹיְבַי נָתַתָּה לִּי עֹרֶף וּמְשַׂנְאַי אַצְמִיתֵם׃ מב יְשַׁוְּעוּ
וְאֵין מוֹשִׁיעַ עַל־יְהֹוָה וְלֹא עָנָם׃ מג וְאֶשְׁחָקֵם כְּעָפָר עַל־
פְּנֵי־רוּחַ כְּטִיט חוּצוֹת אֲרִיקֵם׃ מד תְּפַלְּטֵנִי מֵרִיבֵי עָם
תְּשִׂימֵנִי לְרֹאשׁ גּוֹיִם עַם לֹא־יָדַעְתִּי יַעַבְדוּנִי׃ מה לְשֵׁמַע
אֹזֶן יִשָּׁמְעוּ לִי בְּנֵי־נֵכָר יְכַחֲשׁוּ־לִי׃ מו בְּנֵי־נֵכָר יִבֹּלוּ וְיַחְרְגוּ
מִמִּסְגְּרוֹתֵיהֶם׃ מז חַי־יְהֹוָה וּבָרוּךְ צוּרִי וְיָרוּם אֱלוֹהֵי
יִשְׁעִי׃ מח הָאֵל הַנּוֹתֵן נְקָמוֹת לִי וַיַּדְבֵּר עַמִּים תַּחְתָּי׃
מט מְפַלְּטִי מֵאֹיְבָי אַף מִן־קָמַי תְּרוֹמְמֵנִי מֵאִישׁ חָמָס
תַּצִּילֵנִי׃ נ עַל־כֵּן ׀ אוֹדְךָ בַגּוֹיִם ׀ יְהֹוָה וּלְשִׁמְךָ אֲזַמֵּרָה׃
נא מַגְדִּל [מַגְדִּיל] יְשׁוּעוֹת מַלְכּוֹ וְעֹשֶׂה חֶסֶד ׀ לִמְשִׁיחוֹ
לְדָוִד וּלְזַרְעוֹ עַד־עוֹלָם׃

כ

א לַמְנַצֵּחַ מִזְמוֹר לְדָוִד׃ ב יַעַנְךָ יְהֹוָה בְּיוֹם צָרָה
יְשַׂגֶּבְךָ שֵׁם ׀ אֱלֹהֵי יַעֲקֹב׃ ג יִשְׁלַח־עֶזְרְךָ מִקֹּדֶשׁ וּמִצִּיּוֹן
יִסְעָדֶךָּ׃ ד יִזְכֹּר כָּל־מִנְחֹתֶךָ וְעוֹלָתְךָ יְדַשְּׁנֶה סֶלָה׃ ה יִתֶּן־
לְךָ כִלְבָבֶךָ וְכָל־עֲצָתְךָ יְמַלֵּא׃ ו נְרַנְּנָה ׀ בִּישׁוּעָתֶךָ וּבְשֵׁם־
אֱלֹהֵינוּ נִדְגֹּל יְמַלֵּא יְהֹוָה כָּל־מִשְׁאֲלוֹתֶיךָ׃ ז עַתָּה יָדַעְתִּי
כִּי הוֹשִׁיעַ ׀ יְהֹוָה מְשִׁיחוֹ יַעֲנֵהוּ מִשְּׁמֵי קָדְשׁוֹ בִּגְבֻרוֹת
יֵשַׁע יְמִינוֹ׃ ח אֵלֶּה בָרֶכֶב וְאֵלֶּה בַסּוּסִים וַאֲנַחְנוּ ׀ בְּשֵׁם־

we mention the name of the Lord our God. 9. They kneel and fall, but we rise and gain strength. 10. O Lord, save [us]; may the King answer us on the day we call.

22

Reflections found on page 42

1. For the conductor, on the *Ayeleth Hashachar*, a song of David. 2. My God, my God, why have You forsaken me? [You are] far from my salvation [and] from the words of my moaning. 3. My God, I call out by day and You do not reply, and at night I do not keep silent. 4. But You are holy; You await the praises of Israel. 5. Our ancestors trusted in You; they trusted and You rescued them. 6. They cried out to You and they escaped; they trusted in You and they were not shamed. 7. But I am a worm and not a man; a reproach of man, despised by peoples. 8. All who see me will mock me; they will open their lips, they will shake their head. 9. One should cast his trust upon the Lord, and He will rescue him; He will save him because He delights in him. 10. For You drew me from the womb; You made me secure on my mother's breasts. 11. Upon You, I was cast from birth; from my mother's womb You are my God. 12. Do not distance Yourself from me, for distress is near; for there is none to help. 13. Great bulls have surrounded me; the mighty ones of Bashan encompassed me. 14. They opened their mouth against me [like] a tearing, roaring lion. 15. I was spilled like water, and all my bones were separated; my heart was like wax, melting within my innards. 16. My strength became dried out like a potsherd, and my tongue cleaves to my palate; and You set me down in the dust of death. 17. For dogs have surrounded me; a band of evildoers has encompassed me, like a lion, my hands and feet. 18. I tell about all my bones. They look and gloat over me. 19. They share my garments among themselves and cast lots for my raiment. 20. But You, O Lord, do not distance Yourself; my strength, hasten to my assistance. 21. Save my soul from the sword, my only one from the grip of the dog. 22. Save me from the lion's mouth, as from the horns of the wild oxen You answered me. 23. I will tell Your name to my brothers; in the midst of the congregation I will praise You. 24. You who fear the Lord, praise Him; all the seed of Jacob, honor Him, and fear Him, all the seed of Israel. 25. For He has neither despised nor abhorred the cry of the poor, neither has He hidden His countenance from him; and when he cried out to Him, He hearkened. 26. Because of You is my praise in the great congregation; I pay my vows in the presence of those who fear Him. 27. The humble shall eat and be

יְהוָה אֱלֹהֵינוּ נַזְכִּיר: ט הֵמָּה כָּרְעוּ וְנָפָלוּ וַאֲנַחְנוּ קַּמְנוּ
וַנִּתְעוֹדָד: י יְהוָה הוֹשִׁיעָה הַמֶּלֶךְ יַעֲנֵנוּ בְיוֹם־קָרְאֵנוּ:

כב

א לַמְנַצֵּחַ עַל־אַיֶּלֶת הַשַּׁחַר מִזְמוֹר לְדָוִד: ב אֵלִי
אֵלִי לָמָה עֲזַבְתָּנִי רָחוֹק מִישׁוּעָתִי דִּבְרֵי שַׁאֲגָתִי: ג אֱלֹהַי
אֶקְרָא יוֹמָם וְלֹא תַעֲנֶה וְלַיְלָה וְלֹא־דוּמִיָּה לִי: ד וְאַתָּה
קָדוֹשׁ יוֹשֵׁב תְּהִלּוֹת יִשְׂרָאֵל: ה בְּךָ בָּטְחוּ אֲבֹתֵינוּ בָּטְחוּ
וַתְּפַלְּטֵמוֹ: ו אֵלֶיךָ זָעֲקוּ וְנִמְלָטוּ בְּךָ בָטְחוּ וְלֹא־בוֹשׁוּ:
ז וְאָנֹכִי תוֹלַעַת וְלֹא־אִישׁ חֶרְפַּת אָדָם וּבְזוּי עָם: ח כָּל־
רֹאַי יַלְעִגוּ לִי יַפְטִירוּ בְשָׂפָה יָנִיעוּ רֹאשׁ: ט גֹּל אֶל־יְהוָה
יְפַלְּטֵהוּ יַצִּילֵהוּ כִּי חָפֵץ בּוֹ: י כִּי־אַתָּה גֹחִי מִבָּטֶן מַבְטִיחִי
עַל־שְׁדֵי אִמִּי: יא עָלֶיךָ הָשְׁלַכְתִּי מֵרָחֶם מִבֶּטֶן אִמִּי אֵלִי
אָתָּה: יב אַל־תִּרְחַק מִמֶּנִּי כִּי־צָרָה קְרוֹבָה כִּי־אֵין עוֹזֵר:
יג סְבָבוּנִי פָּרִים רַבִּים אַבִּירֵי בָשָׁן כִּתְּרוּנִי: יד פָּצוּ עָלַי
פִּיהֶם אַרְיֵה טֹרֵף וְשֹׁאֵג: טו כַּמַּיִם נִשְׁפַּכְתִּי וְהִתְפָּרְדוּ כָּל־
עַצְמוֹתָי הָיָה לִבִּי כַּדּוֹנָג נָמֵס בְּתוֹךְ מֵעָי: טז יָבֵשׁ כַּחֶרֶשׂ
| כֹּחִי וּלְשׁוֹנִי מֻדְבָּק מַלְקוֹחָי וְלַעֲפַר־מָוֶת תִּשְׁפְּתֵנִי: יז כִּי־
סְבָבוּנִי כְּלָבִים עֲדַת מְרֵעִים הִקִּיפוּנִי כָּאֲרִי יָדַי וְרַגְלָי: יח
אֲסַפֵּר כָּל־עַצְמוֹתָי הֵמָּה יַבִּיטוּ יִרְאוּ־בִי: יט יְחַלְּקוּ בְגָדַי
לָהֶם וְעַל־לְבוּשִׁי יַפִּילוּ גוֹרָל: כ וְאַתָּה יְהוָה אַל־תִּרְחָק
אֱיָלוּתִי לְעֶזְרָתִי חוּשָׁה: כא הַצִּילָה מֵחֶרֶב נַפְשִׁי מִיַּד־כֶּלֶב
יְחִידָתִי: כב הוֹשִׁיעֵנִי מִפִּי אַרְיֵה וּמִקַּרְנֵי רֵמִים עֲנִיתָנִי:
כג אֲסַפְּרָה שִׁמְךָ לְאֶחָי בְּתוֹךְ קָהָל אֲהַלְלֶךָּ: כד יִרְאֵי
יְהוָה | הַלְלוּהוּ כָּל־זֶרַע יַעֲקֹב כַּבְּדוּהוּ וְגוּרוּ מִמֶּנּוּ כָּל־זֶרַע
יִשְׂרָאֵל: כה כִּי לֹא־בָזָה וְלֹא שִׁקַּץ עֱנוּת עָנִי וְלֹא־הִסְתִּיר
פָּנָיו מִמֶּנּוּ וּבְשַׁוְּעוֹ אֵלָיו שָׁמֵעַ: כו מֵאִתְּךָ תְהִלָּתִי בְּקָהָל רָב

sated; they shall praise the Lord, those who seek him; your hearts shall live forever. 28. All the ends of the earth shall remember and return to the Lord, and all the families of the nations shall prostrate themselves before You. 29. For the kingship is the Lord's, and He rules over the nations. 30. They shall eat all the best of the earth and prostrate themselves; before Him shall all those who descend to the dust kneel, and He will not quicken his soul. 31. The seed that worships Him; it shall be told to the generation concerning the Lord. 32. They shall come and tell His righteousness to the newborn people, that which He has done.

23

Reflections found on page 46

1. A song of David. The Lord is my shepherd; I shall not want. 2. He causes me to lie down in green pastures; He leads me beside still waters. 3. He restores my soul; He leads me in paths of righteousness for His name's sake. 4. Even when I walk in the valley of darkness, I will fear no evil for You are with me; Your rod and Your staff-they comfort me. 5. You set a table before me in the presence of my adversaries; You anointed my head with oil; my cup overflows. 6. May only goodness and kindness pursue me all the days of my life, and I will dwell in the house of the Lord for length of days.

28

Reflections found on page 50

1. Of David. To You, O Lord, I call. My Rock, do not be deaf to me, lest You be silent to me, and I will be likened to those who descend into the Pit. 2. Hearken to the voice of my supplications when I cry out to You, when I lift my hands towards Your Holy Sanctuary. 3. Do not cause me to be drawn with the wicked or with those who work iniquity, who speak peace with their friends but evil is in their heart. 4. Give them according to their deeds and according to the evil of their endeavors; according to the work of their hands give to them; return their recompense to them. 5. For they do not understand the works of the Lord or the deeds of His hands. He shall break them down and not build them up. 6. Blessed is the Lord, for He has heard the voice of my supplication. 7. The Lord is my strength and my shield; my heart trusted in Him and I

נְדָרַי אֲשַׁלֵּם נֶגֶד יְרֵאָיו׃ כז יֹאכְלוּ עֲנָוִים | וְיִשְׂבָּעוּ יְהַלְלוּ
יְהוָה דֹּרְשָׁיו יְחִי לְבַבְכֶם לָעַד׃ כח יִזְכְּרוּ | וְיָשֻׁבוּ אֶל־יְהוָה
כָּל־אַפְסֵי־אָרֶץ וְיִשְׁתַּחֲווּ לְפָנֶיךָ כָּל־מִשְׁפְּחוֹת גּוֹיִם׃ כט
כִּי לַיהוָה הַמְּלוּכָה וּמֹשֵׁל בַּגּוֹיִם׃ ל אָכְלוּ וַיִּשְׁתַּחֲווּ | כָּל־
דִּשְׁנֵי־אֶרֶץ לְפָנָיו יִכְרְעוּ כָּל־יוֹרְדֵי עָפָר וְנַפְשׁוֹ לֹא חִיָּה׃ לא
זֶרַע יַעַבְדֶנּוּ יְסֻפַּר לַאדֹנָי לַדּוֹר׃ לב יָבֹאוּ וְיַגִּידוּ צִדְקָתוֹ
לְעַם נוֹלָד כִּי עָשָׂה׃

כג

א מִזְמוֹר לְדָוִד יְהוָה רֹעִי לֹא אֶחְסָר׃ ב בִּנְאוֹת
דֶּשֶׁא יַרְבִּיצֵנִי עַל־מֵי מְנֻחוֹת יְנַהֲלֵנִי׃ ג נַפְשִׁי יְשׁוֹבֵב יַנְחֵנִי
בְמַעְגְּלֵי־צֶדֶק לְמַעַן שְׁמוֹ׃ ד גַּם כִּי־אֵלֵךְ בְּגֵיא צַלְמָוֶת לֹא־
אִירָא רָע כִּי־אַתָּה עִמָּדִי שִׁבְטְךָ וּמִשְׁעַנְתֶּךָ הֵמָּה יְנַחֲמֻנִי׃
ה תַּעֲרֹךְ לְפָנַי | שֻׁלְחָן נֶגֶד צֹרְרָי דִּשַּׁנְתָּ בַשֶּׁמֶן רֹאשִׁי כּוֹסִי
רְוָיָה׃ ו אַךְ טוֹב וָחֶסֶד יִרְדְּפוּנִי כָּל־יְמֵי חַיָּי וְשַׁבְתִּי בְּבֵית־
יְהוָה לְאֹרֶךְ יָמִים׃

כח

א לְדָוִד אֵלֶיךָ יְהוָה | אֶקְרָא צוּרִי אַל־תֶּחֱרַשׁ
מִמֶּנִּי פֶּן־תֶּחֱשֶׁה מִמֶּנִּי וְנִמְשַׁלְתִּי עִם־יוֹרְדֵי בוֹר׃ ב שְׁמַע
קוֹל תַּחֲנוּנַי בְּשַׁוְּעִי אֵלֶיךָ בְּנָשְׂאִי יָדַי אֶל־דְּבִיר קָדְשֶׁךָ׃ ג
אַל־תִּמְשְׁכֵנִי עִם־רְשָׁעִים וְעִם־פֹּעֲלֵי אָוֶן דֹּבְרֵי שָׁלוֹם עִם־
רֵעֵיהֶם וְרָעָה בִּלְבָבָם׃ ד תֶּן־לָהֶם כְּפָעֳלָם וּכְרֹעַ מַעַלְלֵיהֶם
כְּמַעֲשֵׂה יְדֵיהֶם תֵּן לָהֶם הָשֵׁב גְּמוּלָם לָהֶם׃ ה כִּי לֹא
יָבִינוּ אֶל־פְּעֻלֹּת יְהוָה וְאֶל־מַעֲשֵׂה יָדָיו יֶהֶרְסֵם וְלֹא יִבְנֵם׃
ו בָּרוּךְ יְהוָה כִּי־שָׁמַע קוֹל תַּחֲנוּנָי׃ ז יְהוָה | עֻזִּי וּמָגִנִּי בּוֹ
בָטַח לִבִּי וְנֶעֱזָרְתִּי וַיַּעֲלֹז לִבִּי וּמִשִּׁירִי אֲהוֹדֶנּוּ׃ ח יְהוָה

was helped; my heart rejoiced and I will thank Him with my song. 8. The Lord is strength to them and He is the stronghold of the salvations of His anointed. 9. Save Your people and bless Your inheritance, and tend them and elevate them forever.

30

Reflections found on page 54

1. A psalm; a song of dedication of the House, of David. 2. I will exalt You, O Lord, for You have raised me up, and You have not allowed my enemies to rejoice over me. 3. O Lord, I have cried out to You, and You have healed me. 4. O Lord, You have brought my soul from the grave; You have revived me from my descent into the Pit. 5. Sing to the Lord, His pious ones, and give thanks to His holy name. 6. For His wrath lasts but a moment; life results from His favor; in the evening, weeping may tarry, but in the morning there is joyful singing. 7. And I said in my tranquility, "I will never falter." 8. O Lord, with Your will, You set up my mountain to be might, You hid Your countenance and I became frightened. 9. To You, O Lord, I would call, and to the Lord I would supplicate. 10. "What gain is there in my blood, in my descent to the grave? Will dust thank You; will it recite Your truth? 11. Hear, O Lord, and be gracious to me; O Lord, be my helper." 12. You have turned my lament into dancing for me; You loosened my sackcloth and girded me with joy. 13. So that my soul will sing praises to You and not be silent. O Lord, my God, I will thank You forever.

31

Reflections found on page 58

1. To the conductor, a song of David. 2. I took refuge in You, O Lord; let me not be shamed forever; rescue me with Your righteousness. 3. Incline Your ear to me, quickly rescue me; be a rock of strength to me, a stronghold to save me. 4. For You are my Rock and my Stronghold, and for Your name's sake, You shall lead me and guide me. 5. You shall free me from this net which they have hidden for me, for You are my stronghold. 6. In Your hand I entrust my spirit; You have redeemed me, O Lord, God of truth. 7. I hated those who await worthless vanities, but I hoped for the Lord. 8. I will exult and rejoice in Your kindness, for You have seen my affliction; You have known the troubles of my soul. 9. And you did not deliver me into the hands of an enemy; You have placed my feet in a broad

עֹז־לָמוֹ וּמָעוֹז יְשׁוּעוֹת מְשִׁיחוֹ הוּא׃ ט הוֹשִׁיעָה אֶת־עַמֶּךָ
וּבָרֵךְ אֶת־נַחֲלָתֶךָ וּרְעֵם וְנַשְּׂאֵם עַד־הָעוֹלָם׃

ל

א מִזְמוֹר שִׁיר חֲנֻכַּת הַבַּיִת לְדָוִד׃ ב אֲרוֹמִמְךָ יְהֹוָה כִּי
דִלִּיתָנִי וְלֹא־שִׂמַּחְתָּ אֹיְבַי לִי׃ ג יְהֹוָה אֱלֹהָי שִׁוַּעְתִּי אֵלֶיךָ
וַתִּרְפָּאֵנִי׃ ד יְהֹוָה הֶעֱלִיתָ מִן־שְׁאוֹל נַפְשִׁי חִיִּיתַנִי מִיָּורְדֵי־
[מִיָּרְדִי] בוֹר׃ ה זַמְּרוּ לַיהֹוָה חֲסִידָיו וְהוֹדוּ לְזֵכֶר קָדְשׁוֹ׃
ו כִּי רֶגַע בְּאַפּוֹ חַיִּים בִּרְצוֹנוֹ בָּעֶרֶב יָלִין בֶּכִי וְלַבֹּקֶר רִנָּה׃
ז וַאֲנִי אָמַרְתִּי בְשַׁלְוִי בַּל־אֶמּוֹט לְעוֹלָם׃ ח יְהֹוָה בִּרְצוֹנְךָ
הֶעֱמַדְתָּה לְהַרְרִי עֹז הִסְתַּרְתָּ פָנֶיךָ הָיִיתִי נִבְהָל׃ ט אֵלֶיךָ
יְהֹוָה אֶקְרָא וְאֶל־אֲדֹנָי אֶתְחַנָּן׃ י מַה־בֶּצַע בְּדָמִי בְּרִדְתִּי
אֶל־שָׁחַת הֲיוֹדְךָ עָפָר הֲיַגִּיד אֲמִתֶּךָ׃ יא שְׁמַע־יְהֹוָה וְחָנֵּנִי
יְהֹוָה הֱיֵה עֹזֵר לִי׃ יב הָפַכְתָּ מִסְפְּדִי לְמָחוֹל לִי פִּתַּחְתָּ
שַׂקִּי וַתְּאַזְּרֵנִי שִׂמְחָה׃ יג לְמַעַן ׀ יְזַמֶּרְךָ כָבוֹד וְלֹא יִדֹּם
יְהֹוָה אֱלֹהַי לְעוֹלָם אוֹדֶךָּ׃

לא

א לַמְנַצֵּחַ מִזְמוֹר לְדָוִד׃ ב בְּךָ יְהֹוָה חָסִיתִי
אַל־אֵבוֹשָׁה לְעוֹלָם בְּצִדְקָתְךָ פַלְּטֵנִי׃ ג הַטֵּה אֵלַי ׀
אָזְנְךָ מְהֵרָה הַצִּילֵנִי הֱיֵה לִי ׀ לְצוּר־מָעוֹז לְבֵית מְצוּדוֹת
לְהוֹשִׁיעֵנִי׃ ד כִּי־סַלְעִי וּמְצוּדָתִי אָתָּה וּלְמַעַן שִׁמְךָ תַּנְחֵנִי
וּתְנַהֲלֵנִי׃ ה תּוֹצִיאֵנִי מֵרֶשֶׁת זוּ טָמְנוּ לִי כִּי־אַתָּה מָעוּזִּי׃ ו
בְּיָדְךָ אַפְקִיד רוּחִי פָּדִיתָה אוֹתִי יְהֹוָה אֵל אֱמֶת׃ ז שָׂנֵאתִי
הַשֹּׁמְרִים הַבְלֵי־שָׁוְא וַאֲנִי אֶל־יְהֹוָה בָּטָחְתִּי׃ ח אָגִילָה
וְאֶשְׂמְחָה בְּחַסְדֶּךָ אֲשֶׁר רָאִיתָ אֶת־עָנְיִי יָדַעְתָּ בְּצָרוֹת נַפְשִׁי׃

place. 10. Be gracious to me, O Lord, for I am in distress; my eye is dimmed from anger, my soul and my belly. 11. For my life is spent in grief and my years in sighing; my strength has failed because of my iniquity, and my bones have decayed. 12. From all my tormentors I have become a reproach-and very much so to my neighbors-and fright to my acquaintances; those who see me outside avoid me. 13. I was forgotten like a dead person, out of mind; I was like a lost utensil. 14. For I heard the gossip of many, terror from all sides when they take counsel together against me; they plotted to take my soul. 15. But I trusted in You, O Lord; I said, "You are my God." 16. My times are in Your hands; rescue me from the hands of my enemies and from my pursuers. 17. Cause Your countenance to shine upon Your servant; save me with Your kindness. 18. O Lord, let me not be shamed because I called out to You; let the wicked be shamed, let them be silenced to the grave. 19. Let lying lips become mute, those that speak against a righteous man falsely, with haughtiness and disdain. 20. How great is Your goodness that You have laid away for those who fear You, that You have worked for those who take refuge in You, in the presence of the sons of men! 21. You shall hide them in the secrecy of Your countenance, from bands of men; protect them in a shelter from the strife of tongues. 22. Blessed is the Lord for He has been wondrously kind to me in a besieged city. 23. But I said in my haste, "I have been cut off from before Your eyes," but You heard the voice of my supplications when I cried out to You. 24. Love the Lord, all His pious ones. The Lord guards those who believe [in Him] and He pays with a bowstring him who works with haughtiness. 25. Strengthen yourselves, and He will give your heart courage, all who hope to the Lord.

32

Reflections found on page 62

1. Of David, a *Maskil* praiseworthy is he whose transgression is forgiven, whose sin is concealed. 2. Praiseworthy is the man to whom the Lord ascribes no iniquity and in whose spirit there is no guile. 3. When I was silent, my bones decayed with my moaning all day long. 4. For [both] day and night Your hand is heavy upon me; my freshness was transformed as in the droughts of summer, forever. 5. I would inform You of my sin, and I did not conceal my iniquity; I said, "I will confess my transgressions to the Lord," and You forgave the iniquity of my sin forever. 6. For this let every pious man pray to You at the time that You are found, only about a flood of vast waters [that] should not reach him. 7. You are a shelter for me,

ט וְלֹא הִסְגַּרְתַּנִי בְּיַד־אוֹיֵב הֶעֱמַדְתָּ בַמֶּרְחָב רַגְלָי׃ י חָנֵּנִי
יְהוָה כִּי צַר־לִי עָשְׁשָׁה בְכַעַס עֵינִי נַפְשִׁי וּבִטְנִי׃ יא כִּי כָלוּ
בְיָגוֹן חַיַּי וּשְׁנוֹתַי בַּאֲנָחָה כָּשַׁל בַּעֲוֺנִי כֹחִי וַעֲצָמַי עָשֵׁשׁוּ׃
יב מִכָּל־צֹרְרַי הָיִיתִי חֶרְפָּה וְלִשְׁכֵנַי | מְאֹד וּפַחַד לִמְיֻדָּעָי
רֹאַי בַּחוּץ נָדְדוּ מִמֶּנִּי׃ יג נִשְׁכַּחְתִּי כְּמֵת מִלֵּב הָיִיתִי כִּכְלִי
אֹבֵד׃ יד כִּי שָׁמַעְתִּי | דִּבַּת רַבִּים מָגוֹר מִסָּבִיב בְּהִוָּסְדָם
יַחַד עָלַי לָקַחַת נַפְשִׁי זָמָמוּ׃ טו וַאֲנִי | עָלֶיךָ בָטַחְתִּי יְהוָה
אָמַרְתִּי אֱלֹהַי אָתָּה׃ טז בְּיָדְךָ עִתֹּתָי הַצִּילֵנִי מִיַּד־אוֹיְבַי
וּמֵרֹדְפָי׃ יז הָאִירָה פָנֶיךָ עַל־עַבְדֶּךָ הוֹשִׁיעֵנִי בְחַסְדֶּךָ׃ יח
יְהוָה אַל־אֵבוֹשָׁה כִּי קְרָאתִיךָ יֵבֹשׁוּ רְשָׁעִים יִדְּמוּ לִשְׁאוֹל׃
יט תֵּאָלַמְנָה שִׂפְתֵי שָׁקֶר הַדֹּבְרוֹת עַל־צַדִּיק עָתָק בְּגַאֲוָה
וָבוּז׃ כ מָה רַב טוּבְךָ אֲשֶׁר־צָפַנְתָּ לִּירֵאֶיךָ פָּעַלְתָּ לַחוֹסִים
בָּךְ נֶגֶד בְּנֵי אָדָם׃ כא תַּסְתִּירֵם בְּסֵתֶר פָּנֶיךָ מֵרֻכְסֵי אִישׁ
תִּצְפְּנֵם בְּסֻכָּה מֵרִיב לְשֹׁנוֹת׃ כב בָּרוּךְ יְהוָה כִּי־הִפְלִיא
חַסְדּוֹ לִי בְּעִיר מָצוֹר׃ כג וַאֲנִי | אָמַרְתִּי בְחָפְזִי נִגְרַזְתִּי
מִנֶּגֶד עֵינֶיךָ אָכֵן שָׁמַעְתָּ קוֹל תַּחֲנוּנַי בְּשַׁוְּעִי אֵלֶיךָ׃ כד
אֶהֱבוּ אֶת־יְהוָה כָּל־חֲסִידָיו אֱמוּנִים נֹצֵר יְהוָה וּמְשַׁלֵּם עַל־
יֶתֶר עֹשֵׂה גַאֲוָה׃ כה חִזְקוּ וְיַאֲמֵץ לְבַבְכֶם כָּל־הַמְיַחֲלִים
לַיהוָה׃

לב

א לְדָוִד מַשְׂכִּיל אַשְׁרֵי נְשׂוּי־פֶּשַׁע כְּסוּי חֲטָאָה׃
ב אַשְׁרֵי־אָדָם לֹא יַחְשֹׁב יְהוָה לוֹ עָוֺן וְאֵין בְּרוּחוֹ רְמִיָּה׃
ג כִּי הֶחֱרַשְׁתִּי בָּלוּ עֲצָמָי בְּשַׁאֲגָתִי כָּל־הַיּוֹם׃ ד כִּי | יוֹמָם
וָלַיְלָה | תִּכְבַּד עָלַי יָדֶךָ נֶהְפַּךְ לְשַׁדִּי בְּחַרְבֹנֵי קַיִץ סֶלָה׃ ה
חַטָּאתִי אוֹדִיעֲךָ וַעֲוֺנִי לֹא־כִסִּיתִי אָמַרְתִּי אוֹדֶה עֲלֵי פְשָׁעַי
לַיהוָה וְאַתָּה נָשָׂאתָ עֲוֺן חַטָּאתִי סֶלָה׃ ו עַל־זֹאת יִתְפַּלֵּל
כָּל־חָסִיד | אֵלֶיךָ לְעֵת מְצֹא רַק לְשֵׁטֶף מַיִם רַבִּים אֵלָיו

from an adversary You guard me; with songs of deliverance You encompass me forever, 8. "I will enlighten you and instruct you which way [to go]; I will wink My eye to you." 9. Be not like a horse, like a mule that does not discern; whose mouth must be held with bit and bridle, so that when he is being groomed, he does not come near you. 10. Many are the pains of the wicked, but as for him who trusts in the Lord- kindness will encompass him. 11. Rejoice with the Lord and exult, You righteous, and cause all those of upright hearts to sing praises.

33

Reflections found on page 66

1. Sing praises to the Lord, O you righteous; for the upright, praise is fitting. 2. Give thanks to the Lord with a harp; with a lyre of ten melodies make music to Him. 3. Sing to Him a new song; play well with joyful shouting. 4. For the word of the Lord is upright, and all his deeds are with faith. 5. He loves charity and justice; the earth is full of the Lord's kindness. 6. By the word of the Lord, the heavens were made, and with the breath of His mouth, all their host. 7. He gathers in the water of the sea as a mound; He puts the deeps into treasuries. 8. Let all the earth fear the Lord; let all the inhabitants of the world stand in awe of Him. 9. For He said and it came about; He commanded and it endured. 10. The Lord frustrated the counsel of nations; He put the plans of peoples to nought. 11. The counsel of the Lord shall endure forever; the plans of His heart to all generations. 12. Praiseworthy is the nation whose God is the Lord, the people that He chose as His inheritance. 13. The Lord looked from heaven; He saw all the sons of men. 14. From His dwelling place He oversees all the inhabitants of the earth. 15. He Who forms their hearts together, Who understands all their deeds. 16. The king is not saved with a vast army; a mighty man will not be rescued with great strength. 17. A horse is a false hope for victory, and with his power, he will not escape. 18. Behold the eye of the Lord is to those who fear Him, to those who hope for His kindness, 19. to rescue their soul from death and to sustain them in famine. 20. Our soul waits for the Lord; He is our help and our shield. 21. For our heart will rejoice in Him, because we hoped in His holy name. 22. May Your kindness, O Lord, be upon us, as we hoped for You.

לֹא יַגִּיעוּ: ז אַתָּה | סֵתֶר לִי מִצַּר תִּצְּרֵנִי רָנֵּי פַלֵּט תְּסוֹבְבֵנִי
סֶלָה: ח אַשְׂכִּילְךָ | וְאוֹרְךָ בְּדֶרֶךְ־זוּ תֵלֵךְ אִיעֲצָה עָלֶיךָ
עֵינִי: ט אַל־תִּהְיוּ | כְּסוּס כְּפֶרֶד אֵין הָבִין בְּמֶתֶג וָרֶסֶן עֶדְיוֹ
לִבְלוֹם בַּל קְרֹב אֵלֶיךָ: י רַבִּים מַכְאוֹבִים לָרָשָׁע וְהַבּוֹטֵחַ
בַּיהֹוָה חֶסֶד יְסוֹבְבֶנּוּ: יא שִׂמְחוּ בַיהֹוָה וְגִילוּ צַדִּיקִים
וְהַרְנִינוּ כָּל־יִשְׁרֵי־לֵב:

לג

א רַנְּנוּ צַדִּיקִים בַּיהֹוָה לַיְשָׁרִים נָאוָה תְהִלָּה: ב
הוֹדוּ לַיהֹוָה בְּכִנּוֹר בְּנֵבֶל עָשׂוֹר זַמְּרוּ־לוֹ: ג שִׁירוּ לוֹ שִׁיר
חָדָשׁ הֵיטִיבוּ נַגֵּן בִּתְרוּעָה: ד כִּי־יָשָׁר דְּבַר־יְהֹוָה וְכָל־
מַעֲשֵׂהוּ בֶּאֱמוּנָה: ה אֹהֵב צְדָקָה וּמִשְׁפָּט חֶסֶד יְהֹוָה מָלְאָה
הָאָרֶץ: ו בִּדְבַר יְהֹוָה שָׁמַיִם נַעֲשׂוּ וּבְרוּחַ פִּיו כָּל־צְבָאָם: ז
כֹּנֵס כַּנֵּד מֵי הַיָּם נֹתֵן בְּאֹצָרוֹת תְּהוֹמוֹת: ח יִירְאוּ מֵיְהֹוָה
כָּל־הָאָרֶץ מִמֶּנּוּ יָגוּרוּ כָּל־יֹשְׁבֵי תֵבֵל: ט כִּי הוּא אָמַר וַיֶּהִי
הוּא־צִוָּה וַיַּעֲמֹד: י יְהֹוָה הֵפִיר עֲצַת גּוֹיִם הֵנִיא מַחְשְׁבוֹת
עַמִּים: יא עֲצַת יְהֹוָה לְעוֹלָם תַּעֲמֹד מַחְשְׁבוֹת לִבּוֹ לְדֹר
וָדֹר: יב אַשְׁרֵי הַגּוֹי אֲשֶׁר־יְהֹוָה אֱלֹהָיו הָעָם | בָּחַר לְנַחֲלָה
לוֹ: יג מִשָּׁמַיִם הִבִּיט יְהֹוָה רָאָה אֶת־כָּל־בְּנֵי הָאָדָם: יד
מִמְּכוֹן־שִׁבְתּוֹ הִשְׁגִּיחַ אֶל כָּל־יֹשְׁבֵי הָאָרֶץ: טו הַיֹּצֵר יַחַד
לִבָּם הַמֵּבִין אֶל־כָּל־מַעֲשֵׂיהֶם: טז אֵין הַמֶּלֶךְ נוֹשָׁע בְּרָב־
חָיִל גִּבּוֹר לֹא־יִנָּצֵל בְּרָב־כֹּחַ: יז שֶׁקֶר הַסּוּס לִתְשׁוּעָה וּבְרֹב
חֵילוֹ לֹא יְמַלֵּט: יח הִנֵּה עֵין יְהֹוָה אֶל־יְרֵאָיו לַמְיַחֲלִים
לְחַסְדּוֹ: יט לְהַצִּיל מִמָּוֶת נַפְשָׁם וּלְחַיּוֹתָם בָּרָעָב: כ נַפְשֵׁנוּ
חִכְּתָה לַיהֹוָה עֶזְרֵנוּ וּמָגִנֵּנוּ הוּא: כא כִּי־בוֹ יִשְׂמַח לִבֵּנוּ
כִּי בְשֵׁם קָדְשׁוֹ בָטָחְנוּ: כב יְהִי־חַסְדְּךָ יְהֹוָה עָלֵינוּ כַּאֲשֶׁר
יִחַלְנוּ לָךְ:

37

Reflections found on page 70

1. Of David. Do not compete with the evildoers; do not envy those who commit injustice. 2. For they will be speedily cut off like grass and wither like green vegetation. 3. Trust in the Lord and do good; dwell in the land and be nourished by faith. 4. So shall you delight in the Lord, and He will give you what your heart desires. 5. Commit your way to the Lord, and trust in Him and He will act. 6. And He will reveal your righteousness like the light, and your judgments like noon. 7. Wait for the Lord and hope for Him; do not compete with one whose way prospers, with a man who executes malicious plans. 8. Desist from anger and forsake wrath; do not compete only to do evil. 9. For evildoers shall be cut off, and those who hope for the Lord-they will inherit the land. 10. A short while longer and the wicked man is not here, and you shall look at his place and he is not there. 11. But the humble shall inherit the land, and they shall delight in much peace. 12. The wicked man plots against the righteous and gnashes his teeth at him. 13. The Lord will scoff at him because He saw that his day will come. 14. The wicked initiated war and bent their bow to cast down the poor and the needy, to slay those who walk on a straight path. 15. Their sword shall enter their heart, and their bows shall be broken. 16. The few of the righteous are better than the multitude of many wicked men. 17. For the arms of the wicked shall be broken, but the Lord supports the righteous. 18. The Lord knows the days of the innocent, and their inheritance will be forever. 19. They will not be ashamed in time of calamity, and in days of famine they shall still be satisfied. 20. For the wicked will perish, and the enemies of the Lord are like disappearing light on the plains; they are consumed in smoke, yea they are consumed. 21. A wicked man borrows and does not pay, but the Righteous one is gracious and gives. 22. For those blessed by Him will inherit the land, and those cursed by Him will be cut off. 23. From the Lord a mighty man's steps are established, for He delights in his way. 24. If he falls, he will not be cast down, for the Lord supports his hand. 25. I was young, I also aged, and I have not seen a righteous man forsaken and his seed seeking bread. 26. All day long he is gracious and lends, and his seed is due for a blessing. 27. Shun evil and do good, and dwell forever. 28. For the Lord loves justice, and He shall not forsake His pious ones; they will be guarded forever, but the seed of the wicked shall be cut off. 29. The righteous shall inherit the land and dwell forever in it. 30. The righteous man's mouth utters wisdom, and his tongue speaks judgment. 31. The law of his God is in his heart; his feet do not falter. 32. The wicked man watches for the righteous man and

לז

א לְדָוִד | אַל־תִּתְחַר בַּמְּרֵעִים אַל־תְּקַנֵּא בְּעֹשֵׂי
עַוְלָה׃ ב כִּי כֶחָצִיר מְהֵרָה יִמָּלוּ וּכְיֶרֶק דֶּשֶׁא יִבּוֹלוּן׃ ג
בְּטַח בַּיהוָה וַעֲשֵׂה־טוֹב שְׁכָן־אֶרֶץ וּרְעֵה אֱמוּנָה׃ ד וְהִתְעַנַּג
עַל־יְהוָה וְיִתֶּן־לְךָ מִשְׁאֲלֹת לִבֶּךָ׃ ה גּוֹל עַל־יְהוָה דַּרְכֶּךָ
וּבְטַח עָלָיו וְהוּא יַעֲשֶׂה׃ ו וְהוֹצִיא כָאוֹר צִדְקֶךָ וּמִשְׁפָּטֶךָ
כַּצָּהֳרָיִם׃ ז דּוֹם לַיהוָה וְהִתְחוֹלֵל לוֹ אַל־תִּתְחַר בְּמַצְלִיחַ
דַּרְכּוֹ בְּאִישׁ עֹשֶׂה מְזִמּוֹת׃ ח הֶרֶף מֵאַף וַעֲזֹב חֵמָה אַל־
תִּתְחַר אַךְ־לְהָרֵעַ׃ ט כִּי־מְרֵעִים יִכָּרֵתוּן וְקֹוֵי יְהוָה הֵמָּה
יִירְשׁוּ־אָרֶץ׃ י וְעוֹד מְעַט וְאֵין רָשָׁע וְהִתְבּוֹנַנְתָּ עַל־מְקוֹמוֹ
וְאֵינֶנּוּ׃ יא וַעֲנָוִים יִירְשׁוּ־אָרֶץ וְהִתְעַנְּגוּ עַל־רֹב שָׁלוֹם׃ יב
זֹמֵם רָשָׁע לַצַּדִּיק וְחֹרֵק עָלָיו שִׁנָּיו׃ יג אֲדֹנָי יִשְׂחַק־לוֹ כִּי־
רָאָה כִּי־יָבֹא יוֹמוֹ׃ יד חֶרֶב | פָּתְחוּ רְשָׁעִים וְדָרְכוּ קַשְׁתָּם
לְהַפִּיל עָנִי וְאֶבְיוֹן לִטְבוֹחַ יִשְׁרֵי־דָרֶךְ׃ טו חַרְבָּם תָּבוֹא
בְלִבָּם וְקַשְּׁתוֹתָם תִּשָּׁבַרְנָה׃ טז טוֹב מְעַט לַצַּדִּיק מֵהֲמוֹן
רְשָׁעִים רַבִּים׃ יז כִּי זְרוֹעוֹת רְשָׁעִים תִּשָּׁבַרְנָה וְסוֹמֵךְ
צַדִּיקִים יְהוָה׃ יח יוֹדֵעַ יְהוָה יְמֵי תְמִימִם וְנַחֲלָתָם לְעוֹלָם
תִּהְיֶה׃ יט לֹא־יֵבֹשׁוּ בְּעֵת רָעָה וּבִימֵי רְעָבוֹן יִשְׂבָּעוּ׃ כ כִּי
רְשָׁעִים | יֹאבֵדוּ וְאֹיְבֵי יְהוָה כִּיקַר כָּרִים כָּלוּ בֶעָשָׁן כָּלוּ׃
כא לֹוֶה רָשָׁע וְלֹא יְשַׁלֵּם וְצַדִּיק חוֹנֵן וְנוֹתֵן׃ כב כִּי מְבֹרָכָיו
יִירְשׁוּ אָרֶץ וּמְקֻלָּלָיו יִכָּרֵתוּ׃ כג מֵיְהוָה מִצְעֲדֵי־גֶבֶר כּוֹנָנוּ
וְדַרְכּוֹ יֶחְפָּץ׃ כד כִּי־יִפֹּל לֹא־יוּטָל כִּי־יְהוָה סוֹמֵךְ יָדוֹ׃
כה נַעַר | הָיִיתִי גַּם־זָקַנְתִּי וְלֹא־רָאִיתִי צַדִּיק נֶעֱזָב וְזַרְעוֹ
מְבַקֶּשׁ־לָחֶם׃ כו כָּל־הַיּוֹם חוֹנֵן וּמַלְוֶה וְזַרְעוֹ לִבְרָכָה׃ כז
סוּר מֵרָע וַעֲשֵׂה־טוֹב וּשְׁכֹן לְעוֹלָם׃ כח כִּי יְהוָה | אֹהֵב
מִשְׁפָּט וְלֹא־יַעֲזֹב אֶת־חֲסִידָיו לְעוֹלָם נִשְׁמָרוּ וְזֶרַע רְשָׁעִים
נִכְרָת׃ כט צַדִּיקִים יִירְשׁוּ־אָרֶץ וְיִשְׁכְּנוּ לָעַד עָלֶיהָ׃ ל

seeks to put him to death. 33. The Lord shall not leave him in his hands, and He shall not condemn him [the righteous] when he [the wicked] is judged. 34. Hope to the Lord and keep His way; He will exalt you to inherit the land, and you will witness the destruction of the wicked. 35. I saw a wicked man, powerful, well-rooted as a native who is fresh. 36. And he passed away and behold! he is not here, and I sought him and he was not found. 37. Observe the innocent and see the upright, for there is a future for the man of peace. 38. But transgressors were destroyed together; the future of the wicked was cut off. 39. But the salvation of the righteous is from the Lord, their stronghold in time of distress. 40. The Lord helped them and rescued them; He rescued them from the wicked and saved them because they took refuge in Him.

38

Reflections found on page 74

1. A song of David, to make remembrance. 2. O Lord, do not reprove me with Your anger, nor chastise me with Your wrath. 3. For Your arrows have been shot into me, and Your hand has come down upon me. 4. There is no soundness in my flesh because of Your fury; there is no peace in my bones because of my sin. 5. For my iniquities passed over my head; as a heavy burden they are too heavy for me. 6. My boils are putrid; they fester because of my folly. 7. I am very much stunned and bowed; all day I go around in gloom. 8. For my loins are full of self-effacement; there is no soundness in my flesh. 9. I passed out and was very crushed; I moaned from the turmoil in my heart. 10. O Lord, all my desire is before You, and my sigh is not hidden from You. 11. My heart is engulfed; my strength has left me, and the light of my eyes- they too are not with me. 12. My lovers and my friends stand aloof from my affliction, and those close to me stood afar. 13. And those who seek my life lay traps, and those who seek my harm speak treachery, and all day long they think of deceits. 14. But I am as a deaf person, I do not hear, and like a mute, who does not open his mouth. 15. And I was as a man who does not understand and in whose mouth are no arguments. 16. Because I hoped for You, O Lord; You shall answer, O Lord, my God. 17. For I said, "Lest they rejoice over me; when my foot faltered, they magnified themselves over me." 18. For I am ready for disaster, and my pain is always before me. 19. For I relate my iniquity; I worry about my sin. 20. But my enemies are in the vigor of life, and those

פִּֽי־צַדִּיק יֶהְגֶּה חָכְמָה וּלְשׁוֹנוֹ תְּדַבֵּר מִשְׁפָּט׃ לא תּוֹרַת
אֱלֹהָיו בְּלִבּוֹ לֹא תִמְעַד אֲשֻׁרָיו׃ לב צוֹפֶה רָשָׁע לַצַּדִּיק
וּמְבַקֵּשׁ לַהֲמִיתוֹ׃ לג יְהוָה לֹא־יַעַזְבֶנּוּ בְיָדוֹ וְלֹא יַרְשִׁיעֶנּוּ
בְּהִשָּׁפְטוֹ׃ לד קַוֵּה אֶל־יְהוָה ׀ וּשְׁמֹר דַּרְכּוֹ וִירוֹמִמְךָ
לָרֶשֶׁת אָרֶץ בְּהִכָּרֵת רְשָׁעִים תִּרְאֶה׃ לה רָאִיתִי רָשָׁע עָרִיץ
וּמִתְעָרֶה כְּאֶזְרָח רַעֲנָן׃ לו וַיַּעֲבֹר וְהִנֵּה אֵינֶנּוּ וָאֲבַקְשֵׁהוּ
וְלֹא נִמְצָא׃ לז שְׁמָר־תָּם וּרְאֵה יָשָׁר כִּי־אַחֲרִית לְאִישׁ
שָׁלוֹם׃ לח וּפֹשְׁעִים נִשְׁמְדוּ יַחְדָּו אַחֲרִית רְשָׁעִים נִכְרָתָה׃
לט וּתְשׁוּעַת צַדִּיקִים מֵיְהוָה מָעוּזָּם בְּעֵת צָרָה׃ מ וַיַּעְזְרֵם
יְהוָה וַיְפַלְּטֵם יְפַלְּטֵם מֵרְשָׁעִים וְיוֹשִׁיעֵם כִּי חָסוּ בוֹ׃

לח

א מִזְמוֹר לְדָוִד לְהַזְכִּיר׃ ב יְהוָה אַל־בְּקֶצְפְּךָ
תוֹכִיחֵנִי וּבַחֲמָתְךָ תְיַסְּרֵנִי׃ ג כִּי־חִצֶּיךָ נִחֲתוּ־בִי וַתִּנְחַת
עָלַי יָדֶךָ׃ ד אֵין־מְתֹם בִּבְשָׂרִי מִפְּנֵי זַעְמֶךָ אֵין־שָׁלוֹם בַּעֲצָמַי
מִפְּנֵי חַטָּאתִי׃ ה כִּי־עֲוֺנֹתַי עָבְרוּ רֹאשִׁי כְּמַשָּׂא כָבֵד יִכְבְּדוּ
מִמֶּנִּי׃ ו הִבְאִישׁוּ נָמַקּוּ חַבּוּרֹתָי מִפְּנֵי אִוַּלְתִּי׃ ז נַעֲוֵיתִי
שַׁחֹתִי עַד־מְאֹד כָּל־הַיּוֹם קֹדֵר הִלָּכְתִּי׃ ח כִּי־כְסָלַי מָלְאוּ
נִקְלֶה וְאֵין מְתֹם בִּבְשָׂרִי׃ ט נְפוּגוֹתִי וְנִדְכֵּיתִי עַד־מְאֹד
שָׁאַגְתִּי מִנַּהֲמַת לִבִּי׃ י אֲדֹנָי נֶגְדְּךָ כָל־תַּאֲוָתִי וְאַנְחָתִי
מִמְּךָ לֹא־נִסְתָּרָה׃ יא לִבִּי סְחַרְחַר עֲזָבַנִי כֹחִי וְאוֹר עֵינַי
גַּם־הֵם אֵין אִתִּי׃ יב אֹהֲבַי ׀ וְרֵעַי מִנֶּגֶד נִגְעִי יַעֲמֹדוּ וּקְרוֹבַי
מֵרָחֹק עָמָדוּ׃ יג וַיְנַקְשׁוּ ׀ מְבַקְשֵׁי נַפְשִׁי וְדֹרְשֵׁי רָעָתִי
דִּבְּרוּ הַוּוֹת וּמִרְמוֹת כָּל־הַיּוֹם יֶהְגּוּ׃ יד וַאֲנִי כְחֵרֵשׁ לֹא
אֶשְׁמָע וּכְאִלֵּם לֹא יִפְתַּח־פִּיו׃ טו וָאֱהִי כְּאִישׁ אֲשֶׁר לֹא־
שֹׁמֵעַ וְאֵין בְּפִיו תּוֹכָחוֹת׃ טז כִּי־לְךָ יְהוָה הוֹחָלְתִּי אַתָּה
תַעֲנֶה אֲדֹנָי אֱלֹהָי׃ יז כִּי־אָמַרְתִּי פֶּן־יִשְׂמְחוּ־לִי בְּמוֹט רַגְלִי

who hate me for false reasons have become great. 21. And they repay evil for good; they hate me for my pursuit of goodness. 22. Do not forsake me, O Lord, my God; do not distance Yourself from me. 23. Hasten to my aid, O Lord, my salvation.

39

Reflections found on page 78

1. For the conductor, to *Jeduthun*, a song of David. 2. I said, "I will guard my ways from sinning with my tongue; I will guard my mouth [as with] a muzzle while the wicked man is still before me. 3. I made myself dumb in silence; I was silent from good although my pain was intense. 4. My heart is hot within me; in my thoughts fire burns; I spoke with my tongue, 5. O Lord, let me know my end, and the measure of my days, what it is; I would know when I will cease. 6. Behold You made my days as handbreadths, and my old age is as nought before You; surely all vanity is in every man; this is his condition forever. 7. Man walks but in darkness; all that they stir is but vanity; he gathers yet he knows not who will bring them in. 8. And now, what have I hoped, O Lord? My hope to You is; 9. Save me from all my transgressions; do not make me the reproach of an ignoble man. 10. I have become mute; I will not open my mouth because You have done it. 11. Remove Your affliction from me; from the fear of Your hand I perish. 12. With rebukes for iniquity You have chastised man; You have caused his flesh to decay as by a moth. Surely all man is vanity forever. 13. Hear my prayer, O Lord, and hearken to my cry. Be not silent to my tears, for I am a stranger with You, a dweller as all my forefathers. 14. Turn away from me that I may recover, before I go and am here no longer."

49

Reflections found on page 82

1. For the conductor, by the sons of Korah, a song. 2. Hear this, all you peoples; hearken, all You inhabitants of the earth. 3. Both the sons of "*adam*," and the sons of "*ish*," together rich and poor. 4. My mouth

עָלַי הִגְדִּילוּ: יח כִּי־אֲנִי לְצֶלַע נָכוֹן וּמַכְאוֹבִי נֶגְדִּי תָמִיד:
יט כִּי־עֲוֺנִי אַגִּיד אֶדְאַג מֵחַטָּאתִי: כ וְאֹיְבַי חַיִּים עָצֵמוּ
וְרַבּוּ שֹׂנְאַי שָׁקֶר: כא וּמְשַׁלְּמֵי רָעָה תַּחַת טוֹבָה יִשְׂטְנוּנִי
תַּחַת רָדְופִי [רָדְפִי] ־טוֹב: כב אַל־תַּעַזְבֵנִי יְהֹוָה אֱלֹהַי אַל־
תִּרְחַק מִמֶּנִּי: כג חוּשָׁה לְעֶזְרָתִי אֲדֹנָי תְּשׁוּעָתִי:

לט

א לַמְנַצֵּחַ לידיתון [לִידוּתוּן] מִזְמוֹר לְדָוִד:
ב אָמַרְתִּי אֶשְׁמְרָה דְרָכַי מֵחֲטוֹא בִלְשׁוֹנִי אֶשְׁמְרָה לְפִי
מַחְסוֹם בְּעֹד רָשָׁע לְנֶגְדִּי: ג נֶאֱלַמְתִּי דוּמִיָּה הֶחֱשֵׁיתִי
מִטּוֹב וּכְאֵבִי נֶעְכָּר: ד חַם־לִבִּי | בְּקִרְבִּי בַּהֲגִיגִי תִבְעַר־
אֵשׁ דִּבַּרְתִּי בִּלְשׁוֹנִי: ה הוֹדִיעֵנִי יְהֹוָה | קִצִּי וּמִדַּת יָמַי
מַה־הִיא אֵדְעָה מֶה־חָדֵל אָנִי: ו הִנֵּה טְפָחוֹת | נָתַתָּה יָמַי
וְחֶלְדִּי כְאַיִן נֶגְדֶּךָ אַךְ־כָּל־הֶבֶל כָּל־אָדָם נִצָּב סֶלָה: ז אַךְ־
בְּצֶלֶם | יִתְהַלֶּךְ־אִישׁ אַךְ־הֶבֶל יֶהֱמָיוּן יִצְבֹּר וְלֹא־יֵדַע מִי־
אֹסְפָם: ח וְעַתָּה מַה־קִּוִּיתִי אֲדֹנָי תּוֹחַלְתִּי לְךָ הִיא: ט
מִכָּל־פְּשָׁעַי הַצִּילֵנִי חֶרְפַּת נָבָל אַל־תְּשִׂימֵנִי: י נֶאֱלַמְתִּי לֹא
אֶפְתַּח־פִּי כִּי אַתָּה עָשִׂיתָ: יא הָסֵר מֵעָלַי נִגְעֶךָ מִתִּגְרַת
יָדְךָ אֲנִי כָלִיתִי: יב בְּתוֹכָחוֹת עַל־עָוֺן | יִסַּרְתָּ אִישׁ וַתֶּמֶס
כָּעָשׁ חֲמוּדוֹ אַךְ הֶבֶל כָּל־אָדָם סֶלָה: יג שִׁמְעָה־תְפִלָּתִי |
יְהֹוָה וְשַׁוְעָתִי | הַאֲזִינָה אֶל־דִּמְעָתִי אַל־תֶּחֱרַשׁ כִּי גֵר אָנֹכִי
עִמָּךְ תּוֹשָׁב כְּכָל־אֲבוֹתָי: יד הָשַׁע מִמֶּנִּי וְאַבְלִיגָה בְּטֶרֶם
אֵלֵךְ וְאֵינֶנִּי:

מט

א לַמְנַצֵּחַ | לִבְנֵי־קֹרַח מִזְמוֹר: ב שִׁמְעוּ־זֹאת
כָּל־הָעַמִּים הַאֲזִינוּ כָּל־יֹשְׁבֵי חָלֶד: ג גַּם־בְּנֵי אָדָם גַּם־בְּנֵי־
אִישׁ יַחַד עָשִׁיר וְאֶבְיוֹן: ד פִּי יְדַבֵּר חָכְמוֹת וְהָגוּת לִבִּי

shall speak wisdoms and the thoughts of my heart are understanding. 5. I will bend my ear to a parable; with a lyre, I will solve my riddle. 6. Why should I fear in days of misfortune? The iniquity of my heels surrounds me. 7. Those who rely on their possessions and boast of their great wealth, 8. -a brother cannot redeem a man, he cannot give his ransom to God. 9. The redemption of their soul will be too dear, and unattainable forever. 10. Will he live yet forever and not see the Pit? 11. For he sees that wise men die, together a fool and a boorish man perish, and leave over their possessions to others. 12. In their heart, their houses are forever, their dwellings are for every generation; they call by their names on plots of land. 13. But man does not repose in his glory; he is compared to the silenced animals. 14. This is their way; folly is theirs, and after them they will tell with their mouth forever. 15. Like sheep, they are destined to the grave; death will devour them, and the upright will rule over them in the morning, and their form will outlast the grave as his dwelling place. 16. But God will redeem my soul from the power of the grave, for He shall take me forever. 17. Fear not when a man becomes rich, when the honor of his house increases, 18. For he will not take anything in his death; his glory will not ascend after him. 19. Because in his lifetime he blesses himself, but [all] will praise you, for you will benefit yourself. 20. You shall come to the generation of his forefathers; to eternity they will not see light. 21. Man is in his glory but he does not understand; he is compared to the silenced animals.

56

Reflections found on page 86

1. For the conductor, on *Yonath Elem Rehokim*, of David a *Michtam*, when the Philistines seized him in *Gath*. 2. Be gracious to me, O God, because men yearn to swallow me; all day long the warrior oppresses me. 3. Those who eye me have yearned to swallow me all day long, for many fight against me, O Most High. 4. The day I fear, I will hope to You. 5. With God, I will praise His word; in God I trusted, I will not fear. What can flesh do to me? 6. All day long, my words grieve [me]; all their thoughts about me are for evil. 7. They lodge, they hide, they watch my steps, when they hope for my life. 8. For iniquity, they expect rescue. Bring down nations with anger, O God. 9. You counted my wanderings; place my tears in Your flask. Is it not in Your accounting? 10. Then my enemies will retreat on the day that I call. Thereby I will know that I have a God. 11. With God['s justice] I will praise a word; with the Lord['s kindness] I will

תְּבוּנוֹת׃ ה אַטֶּה לְמָשָׁל אָזְנִי אֶפְתַּח בְּכִנּוֹר חִידָתִי׃ ו לָמָּה
אִירָא בִּימֵי רָע עֲוֹן עֲקֵבַי יְסוּבֵּנִי׃ ז הַבֹּטְחִים עַל־חֵילָם
וּבְרֹב עָשְׁרָם יִתְהַלָּלוּ׃ ח אָח לֹא־פָדֹה יִפְדֶּה אִישׁ לֹא־יִתֵּן
לֵאלֹהִים כָּפְרוֹ׃ ט וְיֵקַר פִּדְיוֹן נַפְשָׁם וְחָדַל לְעוֹלָם׃ י וִיחִי־
עוֹד לָנֶצַח לֹא יִרְאֶה הַשָּׁחַת׃ יא כִּי יִרְאֶה ׀ חֲכָמִים יָמוּתוּ
יַחַד כְּסִיל וָבַעַר יֹאבֵדוּ וְעָזְבוּ לַאֲחֵרִים חֵילָם׃ יב קִרְבָּם
בָּתֵּימוֹ ׀ לְעוֹלָם מִשְׁכְּנֹתָם לְדֹר וָדֹר קָרְאוּ בִשְׁמוֹתָם עֲלֵי
אֲדָמוֹת׃ יג וְאָדָם בִּיקָר בַּל־יָלִין נִמְשַׁל כַּבְּהֵמוֹת נִדְמוּ׃
יד זֶה דַרְכָּם כֵּסֶל לָמוֹ וְאַחֲרֵיהֶם ׀ בְּפִיהֶם יִרְצוּ סֶלָה׃ טו
כַּצֹּאן ׀ לִשְׁאוֹל שַׁתּוּ מָוֶת יִרְעֵם וַיִּרְדּוּ בָם יְשָׁרִים ׀ לַבֹּקֶר
וְצִירָם [וְצוּרָם] לְבַלּוֹת שְׁאוֹל מִזְּבֻל לוֹ׃ טז אַךְ־אֱלֹהִים
יִפְדֶּה נַפְשִׁי מִיַּד־שְׁאוֹל כִּי יִקָּחֵנִי סֶלָה׃ יז אַל־תִּירָא כִּי־
יַעֲשִׁר אִישׁ כִּי־יִרְבֶּה כְּבוֹד בֵּיתוֹ׃ יח כִּי לֹא בְמוֹתוֹ יִקַּח
הַכֹּל לֹא־יֵרֵד אַחֲרָיו כְּבוֹדוֹ׃ יט כִּי־נַפְשׁוֹ בְּחַיָּיו יְבָרֵךְ וְיוֹדֻךָ
כִּי־תֵיטִיב לָךְ׃ כ תָּבוֹא עַד־דּוֹר אֲבוֹתָיו עַד־נֵצַח לֹא יִרְאוּ־
אוֹר׃ כא אָדָם בִּיקָר וְלֹא יָבִין נִמְשַׁל כַּבְּהֵמוֹת נִדְמוּ׃

נו

א לַמְנַצֵּחַ עַל־יוֹנַת אֵלֶם רְחֹקִים לְדָוִד מִכְתָּם
בֶּאֱחֹז אֹתוֹ פְלִשְׁתִּים בְּגַת׃ ב חָנֵּנִי אֱלֹהִים כִּי־שְׁאָפַנִי
אֱנוֹשׁ כָּל־הַיּוֹם לֹחֵם יִלְחָצֵנִי׃ ג שָׁאֲפוּ שׁוֹרְרַי כָּל־הַיּוֹם כִּי־
רַבִּים לֹחֲמִים לִי מָרוֹם׃ ד יוֹם אִירָא אֲנִי אֵלֶיךָ אֶבְטָח׃
ה בֵּאלֹהִים אֲהַלֵּל דְּבָרוֹ בֵּאלֹהִים בָּטַחְתִּי לֹא אִירָא מַה־
יַּעֲשֶׂה בָשָׂר לִי׃ ו כָּל־הַיּוֹם דְּבָרַי יְעַצֵּבוּ עָלַי כָּל־מַחְשְׁבֹתָם
לָרָע׃ ז יָגוּרוּ יִצְפִּינוּ [יִצְפּוֹנוּ] הֵמָּה עֲקֵבַי יִשְׁמֹרוּ כַּאֲשֶׁר
קִוּוּ נַפְשִׁי׃ ח עַל־אָוֶן פַּלֶּט־לָמוֹ בְּאַף עַמִּים ׀ הוֹרֵד אֱלֹהִים׃
ט נֹדִי סָפַרְתָּה אָתָּה שִׂימָה דִמְעָתִי בְנֹאדֶךָ הֲלֹא בְּסִפְרָתֶךָ׃

praise a word. 12. In God I trusted, I will not fear. What can man do to me? 13. Upon me, O God, are Your vows; I will pay thanksgiving offerings to You. 14. For You saved my soul from death, even my feet from stumbling, to walk before God in the light of life.

86

Reflections found on page 90

1. A prayer of David. O Lord, incline Your ear; answer me for I am poor and needy. 2. Watch my soul for I am a pious man; save Your servant-You, my God-who trusts in You. 3. Be gracious to me, O Lord, for I call to You all the days. 4. Cause the soul of Your servant to rejoice, for to You, O Lord, I lift my soul. 5. For You, O Lord, are good and forgiving, with much kindness to all who call You. 6. Lend Your ear, O Lord, to my prayer, and hearken to the voice of my supplications. 7. On the day of my distress I shall call You, for You will answer me. 8. There is none like You among the godly, O Lord, neither is there any like Your works. 9. All nations that You made will come and prostrate themselves before You, O Lord, and glorify Your name. 10. For You are great and perform wonders, You, O God, alone. 11. Teach me Your way, O Lord; I shall walk in Your truth. Unify my heart to fear Your name. 12. I shall thank You, O Lord my God, with all my heart, and I shall glorify Your name forever. 13. For Your kindness is great toward me, and You have saved my soul from the lowest depths of the grave. 14. O God, willful transgressors have risen against me, and a company of mighty ones have sought my life, and they did not place You before themselves. 15. But You, O Lord, are a compassionate and gracious God, slow to anger and with much kindness and truth. 16. Turn to me and be gracious to me; grant Your might to Your servant and save the son of Your maidservant. 17. Grant me a sign for good, and let my enemies see [it] and be ashamed, for You, O Lord, have helped me and comforted me.

88

Reflections found on page 94

1. A song with musical accompaniment of the sons of Korah,

י אָז | יָשׁוּבוּ אוֹיְבַי אָחוֹר בְּיוֹם אֶקְרָא זֶה־יָדַעְתִּי כִּי־
אֱלֹהִים לִי׃ יא בֵּאלֹהִים אֲהַלֵּל דָּבָר בַּיהֹוָה אֲהַלֵּל דָּבָר׃
יב בֵּאלֹהִים בָּטַחְתִּי לֹא אִירָא מַה־יַּעֲשֶׂה אָדָם לִי׃ יג עָלַי
אֱלֹהִים נְדָרֶיךָ אֲשַׁלֵּם תּוֹדֹת לָךְ׃ יד כִּי הִצַּלְתָּ נַפְשִׁי מִמָּוֶת
הֲלֹא רַגְלַי מִדֶּחִי לְהִתְהַלֵּךְ לִפְנֵי אֱלֹהִים בְּאוֹר הַחַיִּים׃

פו

א תְּפִלָּה לְדָוִד הַטֵּה יְהֹוָה אָזְנְךָ עֲנֵנִי כִּי־עָנִי וְאֶבְיוֹן
אָנִי׃ ב שָׁמְרָה נַפְשִׁי כִּי־חָסִיד אָנִי הוֹשַׁע עַבְדְּךָ אַתָּה אֱלֹהַי
הַבּוֹטֵחַ אֵלֶיךָ׃ ג חָנֵּנִי אֲדֹנָי כִּי־אֵלֶיךָ אֶקְרָא כָּל־הַיּוֹם׃ ד
שַׂמֵּחַ נֶפֶשׁ עַבְדֶּךָ כִּי אֵלֶיךָ אֲדֹנָי נַפְשִׁי אֶשָּׂא׃ ה כִּי־אַתָּה
אֲדֹנָי טוֹב וְסַלָּח וְרַב־חֶסֶד לְכָל־קֹרְאֶיךָ׃ ו הַאֲזִינָה יְהֹוָה
תְּפִלָּתִי וְהַקְשִׁיבָה בְּקוֹל תַּחֲנוּנוֹתָי׃ ז בְּיוֹם צָרָתִי אֶקְרָאֶךָּ
כִּי תַעֲנֵנִי׃ ח אֵין־כָּמוֹךָ בָאֱלֹהִים | אֲדֹנָי וְאֵין כְּמַעֲשֶׂיךָ׃ ט
כָּל־גּוֹיִם | אֲשֶׁר עָשִׂיתָ יָבוֹאוּ וְיִשְׁתַּחֲווּ לְפָנֶיךָ אֲדֹנָי וִיכַבְּדוּ
לִשְׁמֶךָ׃ י כִּי־גָדוֹל אַתָּה וְעֹשֵׂה נִפְלָאוֹת אַתָּה אֱלֹהִים
לְבַדֶּךָ׃ יא הוֹרֵנִי יְהֹוָה דַּרְכֶּךָ אֲהַלֵּךְ בַּאֲמִתֶּךָ יַחֵד לְבָבִי
לְיִרְאָה שְׁמֶךָ׃ יב אוֹדְךָ | אֲדֹנָי אֱלֹהַי בְּכָל־לְבָבִי וַאֲכַבְּדָה
שִׁמְךָ לְעוֹלָם׃ יג כִּי־חַסְדְּךָ גָּדוֹל עָלָי וְהִצַּלְתָּ נַפְשִׁי מִשְּׁאוֹל
תַּחְתִּיָּה׃ יד אֱלֹהִים | זֵדִים קָמוּ עָלַי וַעֲדַת עָרִיצִים בִּקְשׁוּ
נַפְשִׁי וְלֹא שָׂמוּךָ לְנֶגְדָּם׃ טו וְאַתָּה אֲדֹנָי אֵל־רַחוּם וְחַנּוּן
אֶרֶךְ אַפַּיִם וְרַב־חֶסֶד וֶאֱמֶת׃ טז פְּנֵה אֵלַי וְחָנֵּנִי תְּנָה־עֻזְּךָ
לְעַבְדֶּךָ וְהוֹשִׁיעָה לְבֶן־אֲמָתֶךָ׃ יז עֲשֵׂה־עִמִּי אוֹת לְטוֹבָה
וְיִרְאוּ שֹׂנְאַי וְיֵבֹשׁוּ כִּי־אַתָּה יְהֹוָה עֲזַרְתַּנִי וְנִחַמְתָּנִי׃

פח

א שִׁיר מִזְמוֹר לִבְנֵי קֹרַח לַמְנַצֵּחַ עַל־מָחֲלַת

for the conductor, about the sick and afflicted one, a *Maskil* of Heman the Ezrahite. 2. O Lord, the God of my salvation! I cried by day; at night I was opposite You. 3. May my prayer come before You; extend Your ear to my supplication. 4. For my soul is sated with troubles, and my life has reached the grave. 5. I was counted with those who descend into the Pit; I was like a man without strength. 6. I am considered among the dead who are free, as the slain who lie in the grave, whom You no longer remember and who were cut off by Your hand. 7. You have put me into the lowest pit, into dark places, into depths. 8. Your wrath lies hard upon me, and [with] all Your waves You have afflicted [me] constantly. 9. You have estranged my friends from me; You have made me an abomination to them; [I am] imprisoned and cannot go out. 10. My eye has failed because of affliction; I have called You every day, I have spread out my palms to You. 11. Will You perform a wonder for the dead? Will the shades rise and thank You forever? 12. Will Your kindness be told in the grave, Your faith in destruction? 13. Will Your wonder be known in the darkness, or Your righteousness in the land of oblivion? 14. As for me, O Lord, I have cried out to You, and in the morning my prayer comes before You. 15. Why, O Lord, do You abandon my soul, do You hide Your countenance from me? 16. I am poor, and close to sudden death; I have borne Your fear, it is well-founded. 17. Your fires of wrath have passed over me; Your terrors have cut me off. 18. They surround me like water all the day; they encompass me together. 19. You have estranged from me lover and friend; my acquaintances are in a place of darkness.

89

Reflections found on page 98

1. A *Maskil* of Ethan the Ezrahite. 2. The kindnesses of the Lord I shall sing forever; to generation after generation I shall make known Your faithfulness, with my mouth. 3. For I said, "Forever will it be built with kindness; as the heavens, with which You will establish Your faithfulness." 4. I formed a covenant with My chosen one; I swore to David My servant. 5. Until eternity, I shall establish your seed, and I shall build your throne for all generations forever. 6. And the heavens acknowledge Your wonder, O Lord, also Your faithfulness in the congregation of holy ones. 7. For who in the heavens is equal to the Lord? [Who] resembles the Lord among the sons of the mighty? 8. God is revered in the great council of the holy ones and feared by all around Him. 9. O Lord, God of Hosts,

לְעַנּוֹת מַשְׂכִּיל לְהֵימָן הָאֶזְרָחִי׃ ב יְהֹוָה אֱלֹהֵי יְשׁוּעָתִי
יוֹם צָעַקְתִּי בַלַּיְלָה נֶגְדֶּךָ׃ ג תָּבוֹא לְפָנֶיךָ תְּפִלָּתִי הַטֵּה־
אָזְנְךָ לְרִנָּתִי׃ ד כִּי־שָׂבְעָה בְרָעוֹת נַפְשִׁי וְחַיַּי לִשְׁאוֹל
הִגִּיעוּ׃ ה נֶחְשַׁבְתִּי עִם־יוֹרְדֵי בוֹר הָיִיתִי כְּגֶבֶר אֵין־אֱיָל׃ ו
בַּמֵּתִים חָפְשִׁי כְּמוֹ חֲלָלִים ׀ שֹׁכְבֵי קֶבֶר אֲשֶׁר לֹא זְכַרְתָּם
עוֹד וְהֵמָּה מִיָּדְךָ נִגְזָרוּ׃ ז שַׁתַּנִי בְּבוֹר תַּחְתִּיּוֹת בְּמַחֲשַׁכִּים
בִּמְצֹלוֹת׃ ח עָלַי סָמְכָה חֲמָתֶךָ וְכָל־מִשְׁבָּרֶיךָ עִנִּיתָ סֶּלָה׃ ט
הִרְחַקְתָּ מְיֻדָּעַי מִמֶּנִּי שַׁתַּנִי תוֹעֵבוֹת לָמוֹ כָּלֻא וְלֹא אֵצֵא׃
י עֵינִי דָאֲבָה מִנִּי עֹנִי קְרָאתִיךָ יְהֹוָה בְּכָל־יוֹם שִׁטַּחְתִּי
אֵלֶיךָ כַפָּי׃ יא הֲלַמֵּתִים תַּעֲשֶׂה־פֶּלֶא אִם־רְפָאִים יָקוּמוּ
יוֹדוּךָ סֶּלָה׃ יב הַיְסֻפַּר בַּקֶּבֶר חַסְדֶּךָ אֱמוּנָתְךָ בָּאֲבַדּוֹן׃ יג
הֲיִוָּדַע בַּחֹשֶׁךְ פִּלְאֶךָ וְצִדְקָתְךָ בְּאֶרֶץ נְשִׁיָּה׃ יד וַאֲנִי ׀ אֵלֶיךָ
יְהֹוָה שִׁוַּעְתִּי וּבַבֹּקֶר תְּפִלָּתִי תְקַדְּמֶךָּ׃ טו לָמָה יְהֹוָה תִּזְנַח
נַפְשִׁי תַּסְתִּיר פָּנֶיךָ מִמֶּנִּי׃ טז עָנִי אֲנִי וְגֹוֵעַ מִנֹּעַר נָשָׂאתִי
אֵמֶיךָ אָפוּנָה׃ יז עָלַי עָבְרוּ חֲרוֹנֶיךָ בִּעוּתֶיךָ צִמְּתוּתֻנִי׃ יח
סַבּוּנִי כַמַּיִם כָּל־הַיּוֹם הִקִּיפוּ עָלַי יָחַד׃ יט הִרְחַקְתָּ מִמֶּנִּי
אֹהֵב וָרֵעַ מְיֻדָּעַי מַחְשָׁךְ׃

פט

א מַשְׂכִּיל לְאֵיתָן הָאֶזְרָחִי׃ ב חַסְדֵי יְהֹוָה
עוֹלָם אָשִׁירָה לְדֹר וָדֹר ׀ אוֹדִיעַ אֱמוּנָתְךָ בְּפִי׃ ג כִּי־אָמַרְתִּי
עוֹלָם חֶסֶד יִבָּנֶה שָׁמַיִם ׀ תָּכִן אֱמוּנָתְךָ בָהֶם׃ ד כָּרַתִּי
בְרִית לִבְחִירִי נִשְׁבַּעְתִּי לְדָוִד עַבְדִּי׃ ה עַד־עוֹלָם אָכִין זַרְעֶךָ
וּבָנִיתִי לְדֹר־וָדוֹר כִּסְאֲךָ סֶלָה׃ ו וְיוֹדוּ שָׁמַיִם פִּלְאֲךָ יְהֹוָה
אַף־אֱמוּנָתְךָ בִּקְהַל קְדֹשִׁים׃ ז כִּי מִי בַשַּׁחַק יַעֲרֹךְ לַיהֹוָה
יִדְמֶה לַיהֹוָה בִּבְנֵי אֵלִים׃ ח אֵל נַעֲרָץ בְּסוֹד־קְדֹשִׁים רַבָּה
וְנוֹרָא עַל־כָּל־סְבִיבָיו׃ ט יְהֹוָה ׀ אֱלֹהֵי צְבָאוֹת מִי־כָמוֹךָ

who is like You, O *Yah*, Who are mighty? And Your faithfulness surrounds You. 10. You rule over the pride of the sea; when it raises its waves, You humble them. 11. You crushed Rahab like one slain; with the arm of Your might You scattered Your enemies. 12. The heaven is Yours, even the earth is Yours; the inhabited earth and the fullness thereof-You founded them. 13. North and south-You created them; Tabor and Hermon sing praises in Your name. 14. You have an arm with might; Your hand is mighty, Your right hand is high. 15. Righteousness and judgment are the basis of Your throne; kindness and truth come before Your countenance. 16. Fortunate is the people that know the blasting of the shofar; O Lord, may they walk in the light of Your countenance. 17. With Your name they rejoice every day, and with Your righteousness they are exalted. 18. For You are the glory of their might, and with Your favor our horns will be raised. 19. For our shield is [devoted] to the Lord, and our king to the Holy One of Israel. 20. Then You spoke in a vision to Your pious ones, and You said, "I placed help on a mighty man; I lifted up a chosen one from the people. 21. I found David My servant, I anointed him with My holy oil. 22. With whom My hand will be established, even My arm will strengthen him. 23. No enemy will exact from him, neither will an unjust person afflict him. 24. And I shall crush his adversaries from before him, and I shall strike his enemies. 25. My faithfulness and My kindness will be with him, and with My name his horn will be raised. 26. I shall place his hand over the sea, and his right hand over the rivers. 27. He will call to Me, 'You are my Father, my God, and the Rock of my salvation.' 28. I, too, shall make him a firstborn, the highest of the kings of the earth. 29. I will forever keep My kindness for him, and My covenant will remain true to him. 30. And I shall make his seed endure forever, and his throne as the days of the heavens. 31. If his sons forsake My Torah and do not walk in My judgments, 32. If they profane My statutes and do not keep My commandments, 33. I shall punish their transgression with a rod, and their iniquity with stripes. 34. But I shall not cancel My kindness from him, and I shall not betray My faith. 35. I shall not profane My covenant, neither shall I alter the utterance of My lips. 36. One thing have I sworn by My holiness, that I will not fail David. 37. His seed will be forever and his throne is like the sun before Me. 38. Like the moon, which is established forever, and it is a witness in the sky, eternally true." 39. But You abandoned and You rejected; You became wroth with Your anointed. 40. You abrogated the covenant of Your servant; You profaned his crown to the ground. 41. You breached all his fences; You made his fortifications a ruin. 42. All wayfarers have plundered him; he was a disgrace to his neighbors. 43. You raised the right hand of his adversaries; You caused

חֲסִין ׀ יָהּ וֶאֱמוּנָתְךָ סְבִיבוֹתֶיךָ׃ י אַתָּה מוֹשֵׁל בְּגֵאוּת
הַיָּם בְּשׂוֹא גַלָּיו אַתָּה תְשַׁבְּחֵם׃ יא אַתָּה דִכִּאתָ כֶחָלָל
רָהַב בִּזְרוֹעַ עֻזְּךָ פִּזַּרְתָּ אוֹיְבֶיךָ׃ יב לְךָ שָׁמַיִם אַף־לְךָ אָרֶץ
תֵּבֵל וּמְלֹאָהּ אַתָּה יְסַדְתָּם׃ יג צָפוֹן וְיָמִין אַתָּה בְרָאתָם
תָּבוֹר וְחֶרְמוֹן בְּשִׁמְךָ יְרַנֵּנוּ׃ יד לְךָ זְרוֹעַ עִם־גְּבוּרָה תָּעֹז
יָדְךָ תָּרוּם יְמִינֶךָ׃ טו צֶדֶק וּמִשְׁפָּט מְכוֹן כִּסְאֶךָ חֶסֶד
וֶאֱמֶת יְקַדְּמוּ פָנֶיךָ׃ טז אַשְׁרֵי הָעָם יוֹדְעֵי תְרוּעָה יְהוָה
בְּאוֹר־פָּנֶיךָ יְהַלֵּכוּן׃ יז בְּשִׁמְךָ יְגִילוּן כָּל־הַיּוֹם וּבְצִדְקָתְךָ
יָרוּמוּ׃ יח כִּי־תִפְאֶרֶת עֻזָּמוֹ אָתָּה וּבִרְצֹנְךָ תָּרִים [תָּרוּם]
קַרְנֵנוּ׃ יט כִּי לַיהוָה מָגִנֵּנוּ וְלִקְדוֹשׁ יִשְׂרָאֵל מַלְכֵּנוּ׃ כ
אָז דִּבַּרְתָּ־בְחָזוֹן לַחֲסִידֶיךָ וַתֹּאמֶר שִׁוִּיתִי עֵזֶר עַל־גִּבּוֹר
הֲרִימוֹתִי בָחוּר מֵעָם׃ כא מָצָאתִי דָּוִד עַבְדִּי בְּשֶׁמֶן קָדְשִׁי
מְשַׁחְתִּיו׃ כב אֲשֶׁר יָדִי תִּכּוֹן עִמּוֹ אַף־זְרוֹעִי תְאַמְּצֶנּוּ׃ כג
לֹא־יַשִּׁא אוֹיֵב בּוֹ וּבֶן־עַוְלָה לֹא יְעַנֶּנּוּ׃ כד וְכַתּוֹתִי מִפָּנָיו
צָרָיו וּמְשַׂנְאָיו אֶגּוֹף׃ כה וֶאֱמוּנָתִי וְחַסְדִּי עִמּוֹ וּבִשְׁמִי
תָּרוּם קַרְנוֹ׃ כו וְשַׂמְתִּי בַיָּם יָדוֹ וּבַנְּהָרוֹת יְמִינוֹ׃ כז הוּא
יִקְרָאֵנִי אָבִי אָתָּה אֵלִי וְצוּר יְשׁוּעָתִי׃ כח אַף־אָנִי בְּכוֹר
אֶתְּנֵהוּ עֶלְיוֹן לְמַלְכֵי־אָרֶץ׃ כט לְעוֹלָם אֶשְׁמָור [אֶשְׁמָר]־לוֹ
חַסְדִּי וּבְרִיתִי נֶאֱמֶנֶת לוֹ׃ ל וְשַׂמְתִּי לָעַד זַרְעוֹ וְכִסְאוֹ כִּימֵי
שָׁמָיִם׃ לא אִם־יַעַזְבוּ בָנָיו תּוֹרָתִי וּבְמִשְׁפָּטַי לֹא יֵלֵכוּן׃
לב אִם־חֻקֹּתַי יְחַלֵּלוּ וּמִצְוֹתַי לֹא יִשְׁמֹרוּ׃ לג וּפָקַדְתִּי
בְשֵׁבֶט פִּשְׁעָם וּבִנְגָעִים עֲוֺנָם׃ לד וְחַסְדִּי לֹא־אָפִיר מֵעִמּוֹ
וְלֹא אֲשַׁקֵּר בֶּאֱמוּנָתִי׃ לה לֹא־אֲחַלֵּל בְּרִיתִי וּמוֹצָא שְׂפָתַי
לֹא אֲשַׁנֶּה׃ לו אַחַת נִשְׁבַּעְתִּי בְקָדְשִׁי אִם־לְדָוִד אֲכַזֵּב׃
לז זַרְעוֹ לְעוֹלָם יִהְיֶה וְכִסְאוֹ כַשֶּׁמֶשׁ נֶגְדִּי׃ לח כְּיָרֵחַ יִכּוֹן
עוֹלָם וְעֵד בַּשַּׁחַק נֶאֱמָן סֶלָה׃ לט וְאַתָּה זָנַחְתָּ וַתִּמְאָס
הִתְעַבַּרְתָּ עִם־מְשִׁיחֶךָ׃ מ נֵאַרְתָּה בְּרִית עַבְדֶּךָ חִלַּלְתָּ
לָאָרֶץ נִזְרוֹ׃ מא פָּרַצְתָּ כָל־גְּדֵרֹתָיו שַׂמְתָּ מִבְצָרָיו מְחִתָּה׃

all his enemies to rejoice. 44. You even turned back the sharp edge of his sword, and You did not raise him up in battle. 45. You have brought an end to his shining, and his throne You have cast down to earth. 46. You have shortened the days of his youth; You have enwrapped him with shame forever. 47. How long, O Lord? Will You hide forever? Will Your anger burn like fire? 48. I am mindful what my old age is; for what futility have You created all the sons of man? 49. Who is a man who will live and not see death, who will rescue his soul from the grasp of the grave forever? 50. Where are Your former acts of kindness, O Lord, which You swore to David in your trust? 51. Remember, O Lord, the disgrace of Your servants, which I bear in my bosom, [the disgrace] of all great nations. 52. Which Your enemies disgraced, O Lord, which they disgraced the ends of Your anointed. 53. Blessed is the Lord forever. Amen and Amen.

90

Reflections found on page 102

1. A prayer of Moses, the man of God. O Lord, You have been our dwelling place throughout all generations. 2. Before the mountains were born, and You brought forth the earth and the inhabited world, and from everlasting to everlasting, You are God. 3. You bring man to the crushing point, and You say, "Return, O sons of men." 4. For a thousand years are in Your eyes like yesterday, which passed, and a watch in the night. 5. You carry them away as a flood; they are like a sleep; in the morning, like grass it passes away. 6. In the morning, it blossoms and passes away; in the evening, it is cut off and withers. 7. For we perish from Your wrath, and from Your anger we are dismayed. 8. You have placed our iniquities before You, [the sins of] our youth before the light of Your countenance. 9. For all our days have passed away in Your anger; we have consumed our years as a murmur. 10. The days of our years because of them are seventy years, and if with increase, eighty years; but their pride is toil and pain, for it passes quickly and we fly away. 11. Who knows the might of Your wrath, and according to Your fear is Your anger. 12. So teach the number of our days, so that we shall acquire a heart of wisdom. 13. Return, O Lord, how long? And repent about Your servants. 14. Satiate us in the morning with Your loving-kindness, and let us sing praises and rejoice with all our days. 15. Cause us to rejoice according to the days that You afflicted us, the years that we saw evil. 16. May Your works appear to Your servants, and Your

מב שַׁסֻּהוּ כׇּל־עֹבְרֵי דָרֶךְ הָיָה חֶרְפָּה לִשְׁכֵנָיו : מג הֲרִימוֹתָ
יְמִין צָרָיו הִשְׂמַחְתָּ כׇּל־אוֹיְבָיו : מד אַף־תָּשִׁיב צוּר חַרְבּוֹ
וְלֹא הֲקֵימֹתוֹ בַּמִּלְחָמָה : מה הִשְׁבַּתָּ מִטְּהָרוֹ וְכִסְאוֹ לָאָרֶץ
מִגַּרְתָּה : מו הִקְצַרְתָּ יְמֵי עֲלוּמָיו הֶעֱטִיתָ עָלָיו בּוּשָׁה סֶלָה :
מז עַד־מָה יְהֹוָה תִּסָּתֵר לָנֶצַח תִּבְעַר כְּמוֹ־אֵשׁ חֲמָתֶךָ : מח
זְכׇר־אֲנִי מֶה־חָלֶד עַל־מַה־שָּׁוְא בָּרָאתָ כׇל־בְּנֵי־אָדָם : מט מִי
גֶבֶר יִחְיֶה וְלֹא יִרְאֶה־מָּוֶת יְמַלֵּט נַפְשׁוֹ מִיַּד־שְׁאוֹל סֶלָה : נ
אַיֵּה חֲסָדֶיךָ הָרִאשֹׁנִים | אֲדֹנָי נִשְׁבַּעְתָּ לְדָוִד בֶּאֱמוּנָתֶךָ :
נא זְכֹר אֲדֹנָי חֶרְפַּת עֲבָדֶיךָ שְׂאֵתִי בְחֵיקִי כׇּל־רַבִּים עַמִּים :
נב אֲשֶׁר חֵרְפוּ אוֹיְבֶיךָ | יְהֹוָה אֲשֶׁר חֵרְפוּ עִקְּבוֹת מְשִׁיחֶךָ :
נג בָּרוּךְ יְהֹוָה לְעוֹלָם אָמֵן | וְאָמֵן :

צ

א תְּפִלָּה לְמֹשֶׁה אִישׁ־הָאֱלֹהִים אֲדֹנָי מָעוֹן אַתָּה הָיִיתָ
לָּנוּ בְּדֹר וָדֹר : ב בְּטֶרֶם | הָרִים יֻלָּדוּ וַתְּחוֹלֵל אֶרֶץ וְתֵבֵל
וּמֵעוֹלָם עַד־עוֹלָם אַתָּה אֵל : ג תָּשֵׁב אֱנוֹשׁ עַד־דַּכָּא וַתֹּאמֶר
שׁוּבוּ בְנֵי־אָדָם : ד כִּי אֶלֶף שָׁנִים בְּעֵינֶיךָ כְּיוֹם אֶתְמוֹל
כִּי יַעֲבֹר וְאַשְׁמוּרָה בַלָּיְלָה : ה זְרַמְתָּם שֵׁנָה יִהְיוּ בַּבֹּקֶר
כֶּחָצִיר יַחֲלֹף : ו בַּבֹּקֶר יָצִיץ וְחָלָף לָעֶרֶב יְמוֹלֵל וְיָבֵשׁ : ז
כִּי־כָלִינוּ בְאַפֶּךָ וּבַחֲמָתְךָ נִבְהָלְנוּ : ח שַׁתָּ [שַׁתָּה] עֲוֺנֹתֵינוּ
לְנֶגְדֶּךָ עֲלֻמֵנוּ לִמְאוֹר פָּנֶיךָ : ט כִּי כׇל־יָמֵינוּ פָּנוּ בְעֶבְרָתֶךָ
כִּלִּינוּ שָׁנֵינוּ כְמוֹ־הֶגֶה : י יְמֵי שְׁנוֹתֵינוּ | בָהֶם שִׁבְעִים שָׁנָה
וְאִם בִּגְבוּרֹת | שְׁמוֹנִים שָׁנָה וְרׇהְבָּם עָמָל וָאָוֶן כִּי־גָז חִישׁ
וַנָּעֻפָה : יא מִי־יוֹדֵעַ עֹז אַפֶּךָ וּכְיִרְאָתְךָ עֶבְרָתֶךָ : יב לִמְנוֹת
יָמֵינוּ כֵּן הוֹדַע וְנָבִא לְבַב חׇכְמָה : יג שׁוּבָה יְהֹוָה עַד־מָתָי
וְהִנָּחֵם עַל־עֲבָדֶיךָ : יד שַׂבְּעֵנוּ בַבֹּקֶר חַסְדֶּךָ וּנְרַנְּנָה וְנִשְׂמְחָה
בְּכׇל־יָמֵינוּ : טו שַׂמְּחֵנוּ כִּימוֹת עִנִּיתָנוּ שְׁנוֹת רָאִינוּ רָעָה :
טז יֵרָאֶה אֶל־עֲבָדֶיךָ פׇעֳלֶךָ וַהֲדָרְךָ עַל־בְּנֵיהֶם : יז וִיהִי |

beauty to their sons. 17. And may the pleasantness of the Lord our God be upon us, and the work of our hands establish for us, and the work of our hands establish it.

91

Reflections found on page 106

1. He who dwells in the covert of the Most High will lodge in the shadow of the Almighty. 2. I shall say of the Lord [that He is] my shelter and my fortress, my God in Whom I trust. 3. For He will save you from the snare that traps from the devastating pestilence. 4. With His wing He will cover you, and under His wings you will take refuge; His truth is an encompassing shield. 5. You will not fear the fright of night, the arrow that flies by day; 6. Pestilence that prowls in darkness, destruction that ravages at noon. 7. A thousand will be stationed at your side, and ten thousand at your right hand; but it will not approach you. 8. You will but gaze with your eyes, and you will see the annihilation of the wicked. 9. For you [said], "The Lord is my refuge"; the Most High you made your dwelling. 10. No harm will befall you, nor will a plague draw near to your tent. 11. For He will command His angels on your behalf to guard you in all your ways. 12. On [their] hands they will bear you, lest your foot stumble on a stone. 13. On a young lion and a cobra you will tread; you will trample the young lion and the serpent. 14. For he yearns for Me, and I shall rescue him; I shall fortify him because he knows My name. 15. He will call Me and I shall answer him; I am with him in distress; I shall rescue him and I shall honor him. 16. With length of days I shall satiate him, and I shall show him My salvation.

102

Reflections found on page 110

1. A prayer for a poor man when he enwraps himself and pours out his speech before the Lord. 2. O Lord, hearken to my prayer, and may my cry come to You. 3. Do not hide Your countenance from me; on the day of my distress extend Your ear to me; on the day I call, answer me quickly. 4. For my days have ended in smoke, and as a hearth my bones are dried up. 5. Beaten like grass and withered is my heart, for I have forgotten to eat my bread. 6. From the sound of my sigh my bones clung to my flesh. 7. I was like a bird of the wilderness; I was like an owl of the

נֹעַם אֲדֹנָי אֱלֹהֵינוּ עָלֵינוּ וּמַעֲשֵׂה יָדֵינוּ כּוֹנְנָה עָלֵינוּ וּמַעֲשֵׂה
יָדֵינוּ כּוֹנְנֵהוּ׃

צא

א יֹשֵׁב בְּסֵתֶר עֶלְיוֹן בְּצֵל שַׁדַּי יִתְלוֹנָן׃ ב אֹמַר
לַיהֹוָה מַחְסִי וּמְצוּדָתִי אֱלֹהַי אֶבְטַח־בּוֹ׃ ג כִּי הוּא יַצִּילְךָ
מִפַּח יָקוּשׁ מִדֶּבֶר הַוּוֹת׃ ד בְּאֶבְרָתוֹ | יָסֶךְ לָךְ וְתַחַת כְּנָפָיו
תֶּחְסֶה צִנָּה וְסֹחֵרָה אֲמִתּוֹ׃ ה לֹא־תִירָא מִפַּחַד לָיְלָה מֵחֵץ
יָעוּף יוֹמָם׃ ו מִדֶּבֶר בָּאֹפֶל יַהֲלֹךְ מִקֶּטֶב יָשׁוּד צָהֳרָיִם׃ ז
יִפֹּל מִצִּדְּךָ | אֶלֶף וּרְבָבָה מִימִינֶךָ אֵלֶיךָ לֹא יִגָּשׁ׃ ח רַק
בְּעֵינֶיךָ תַבִּיט וְשִׁלֻּמַת רְשָׁעִים תִּרְאֶה׃ ט כִּי־אַתָּה יְהֹוָה
מַחְסִי עֶלְיוֹן שַׂמְתָּ מְעוֹנֶךָ׃ י לֹא־תְאֻנֶּה אֵלֶיךָ רָעָה וְנֶגַע
לֹא־יִקְרַב בְּאָהֳלֶךָ׃ יא כִּי מַלְאָכָיו יְצַוֶּה־לָּךְ לִשְׁמָרְךָ בְּכָל־
דְּרָכֶיךָ׃ יב עַל־כַּפַּיִם יִשָּׂאוּנְךָ פֶּן־תִּגֹּף בָּאֶבֶן רַגְלֶךָ׃ יג
עַל־שַׁחַל וָפֶתֶן תִּדְרֹךְ תִּרְמֹס כְּפִיר וְתַנִּין׃ יד כִּי בִי חָשַׁק
וַאֲפַלְּטֵהוּ אֲשַׂגְּבֵהוּ כִּי־יָדַע שְׁמִי׃ טו יִקְרָאֵנִי | וְאֶעֱנֵהוּ עִמּוֹ
אָנֹכִי בְצָרָה אֲחַלְּצֵהוּ וַאֲכַבְּדֵהוּ׃ טז אֹרֶךְ יָמִים אַשְׂבִּיעֵהוּ
וְאַרְאֵהוּ בִּישׁוּעָתִי׃

קב

א תְּפִלָּה לְעָנִי כִי־יַעֲטֹף וְלִפְנֵי יְהֹוָה יִשְׁפֹּךְ שִׂיחוֹ׃
ב יְהֹוָה שִׁמְעָה תְפִלָּתִי וְשַׁוְעָתִי אֵלֶיךָ תָבוֹא׃ ג אַל־תַּסְתֵּר
פָּנֶיךָ | מִמֶּנִּי בְּיוֹם צַר לִי הַטֵּה־אֵלַי אָזְנֶךָ בְּיוֹם אֶקְרָא מַהֵר
עֲנֵנִי׃ ד כִּי־כָלוּ בְעָשָׁן יָמָי וְעַצְמוֹתַי כְּמוֹקֵד נִחָרוּ׃ ה הוּכָּה־
כָעֵשֶׂב וַיִּבַשׁ לִבִּי כִּי־שָׁכַחְתִּי מֵאֲכֹל לַחְמִי׃ ו מִקּוֹל אַנְחָתִי
דָּבְקָה עַצְמִי לִבְשָׂרִי׃ ז דָּמִיתִי לִקְאַת מִדְבָּר הָיִיתִי כְּכוֹס

wasteland. 8. I pondered, and I am like a lonely bird on a roof. 9. All day long my enemies revile me; those who scorn me swear by me. 10. For ashes I ate like bread, and my drinks I mixed with weeping. 11. Because of Your fury and Your anger, for You picked me up and cast me down. 12. My days are like a lengthening shadow, and I dry out like grass. 13. But You, O Lord, will be enthroned forever, and Your mention is to all generations. 14. You will rise, You will have mercy on Zion for there is a time to favor it, for the appointed season has arrived. 15. For Your servants desired its stones and favored its dust. 16. And the nations will fear the name of the Lord, and all the kings of the earth Your glory. 17. For the Lord has built up Zion; He has appeared in His glory. 18. He has turned to the prayer of those who cried out, and He did not despise their prayer. 19. Let this be inscribed for the latest generation, and a [newly] created people will praise Yah. 20. For He has looked down from His holy height; the Lord looked from heaven to earth, 21. To hear the cry of the prisoner, to loose the sons of the dying nation; 22. To proclaim in Zion the name of the Lord and His praise in Jerusalem. 23. When peoples gather together, and kingdoms, to serve the Lord. 24. He has afflicted my strength on the way; He has shortened my days. 25. I say, "My God, do not take me away in the middle of my days, You Whose years endure throughout all generations. 26. In the beginning You founded the earth, and the heavens are the work of Your hands. 27. They will perish but You will endure, and all of them will rot away like a garment; like raiment You will turn them over and they will pass away. 28. But You are He, and Your years will not end. 29. The children of Your servants will dwell, and their seed will be established before You."

103

Reflections found on page 114

1. Of David. My soul, bless the Lord, and all my innards, His holy name. 2. My soul, bless the Lord and do not forget any of His benefits. 3. Who forgives all your iniquity, Who heals all your illnesses. 4. Who redeems your life from the pit, Who crowns you with kindness and mercy. 5. Who sates your mouth with goodness, that your youth renews itself like the eagle. 6. The Lord performs charitable deeds and judgment for all oppressed people. 7. He makes His ways known to Moses, to the children of Israel His deeds. 8. The Lord is merciful and gracious, slow to anger and with much kindness. 9. He will not quarrel to eternity, and He will not bear a grudge forever. 10. He has not dealt with us according

חֳרָבוֹת׃ ח שָׁקַדְתִּי וָאֶהְיֶה כְּצִפּוֹר בּוֹדֵד עַל־גָּג׃ ט כָּל־הַיּוֹם
חֵרְפוּנִי אוֹיְבָי מְהוֹלָלַי בִּי נִשְׁבָּעוּ׃ י כִּי אֵפֶר כַּלֶּחֶם אָכָלְתִּי
וְשִׁקֻּוַי בִּבְכִי מָסָכְתִּי׃ יא מִפְּנֵי־זַעַמְךָ וְקִצְפֶּךָ כִּי נְשָׂאתַנִי
וַתַּשְׁלִיכֵנִי׃ יב יָמַי כְּצֵל נָטוּי וַאֲנִי כָּעֵשֶׂב אִיבָשׁ׃ יג וְאַתָּה
יְהוָה לְעוֹלָם תֵּשֵׁב וְזִכְרְךָ לְדֹר וָדֹר׃ יד אַתָּה תָקוּם תְּרַחֵם
צִיּוֹן כִּי עֵת לְחֶנְנָהּ כִּי בָא מוֹעֵד׃ טו כִּי־רָצוּ עֲבָדֶיךָ אֶת־
אֲבָנֶיהָ וְאֶת־עֲפָרָהּ יְחֹנֵנוּ׃ טז וְיִירְאוּ גוֹיִם אֶת־שֵׁם יְהוָה
וְכָל־מַלְכֵי הָאָרֶץ אֶת־כְּבוֹדֶךָ׃ יז כִּי־בָנָה יְהוָה צִיּוֹן נִרְאָה
בִּכְבוֹדוֹ׃ יח פָּנָה אֶל־תְּפִלַּת הָעַרְעָר וְלֹא־בָזָה אֶת־תְּפִלָּתָם׃
יט תִּכָּתֶב זֹאת לְדוֹר אַחֲרוֹן וְעַם נִבְרָא יְהַלֶּל־יָהּ׃ כ כִּי־
הִשְׁקִיף מִמְּרוֹם קָדְשׁוֹ יְהוָה מִשָּׁמַיִם ׀ אֶל־אֶרֶץ הִבִּיט׃
כא לִשְׁמֹעַ אֶנְקַת אָסִיר לְפַתֵּחַ בְּנֵי תְמוּתָה׃ כב לְסַפֵּר
בְּצִיּוֹן שֵׁם יְהוָה וּתְהִלָּתוֹ בִּירוּשָׁלָם׃ כג בְּהִקָּבֵץ עַמִּים
יַחְדָּו וּמַמְלָכוֹת לַעֲבֹד אֶת־יְהוָה׃ כד עִנָּה בַדֶּרֶךְ כֹּחוֹ [כֹּחִי]
קִצַּר יָמָי׃ כה אֹמַר אֵלִי אַל־תַּעֲלֵנִי בַּחֲצִי יָמָי בְּדוֹר דּוֹרִים
שְׁנוֹתֶיךָ׃ כו לְפָנִים הָאָרֶץ יָסַדְתָּ וּמַעֲשֵׂה יָדֶיךָ שָׁמָיִם׃
כז הֵמָּה ׀ יֹאבֵדוּ וְאַתָּה תַעֲמֹד וְכֻלָּם כַּבֶּגֶד יִבְלוּ כַּלְּבוּשׁ
תַּחֲלִיפֵם וְיַחֲלֹפוּ׃ כח וְאַתָּה־הוּא וּשְׁנוֹתֶיךָ לֹא יִתָּמּוּ׃ כט
בְּנֵי־עֲבָדֶיךָ יִשְׁכּוֹנוּ וְזַרְעָם לְפָנֶיךָ יִכּוֹן׃

קג

א לְדָוִד ׀ בָּרְכִי נַפְשִׁי אֶת־יְהוָה וְכָל־קְרָבַי
אֶת־שֵׁם קָדְשׁוֹ׃ ב בָּרְכִי נַפְשִׁי אֶת־יְהוָה וְאַל־תִּשְׁכְּחִי
כָּל־גְּמוּלָיו׃ ג הַסֹּלֵחַ לְכָל־עֲוֹנֵכִי הָרֹפֵא לְכָל־תַּחֲלֻאָיְכִי׃
ד הַגּוֹאֵל מִשַּׁחַת חַיָּיְכִי הַמְעַטְּרֵכִי חֶסֶד וְרַחֲמִים׃ ה
הַמַּשְׂבִּיַע בַּטּוֹב עֶדְיֵךְ תִּתְחַדֵּשׁ כַּנֶּשֶׁר נְעוּרָיְכִי׃ ו עֹשֵׂה
צְדָקוֹת יְהוָה וּמִשְׁפָּטִים לְכָל־עֲשׁוּקִים׃ ז יוֹדִיעַ דְּרָכָיו
לְמֹשֶׁה לִבְנֵי יִשְׂרָאֵל עֲלִילוֹתָיו׃ ח רַחוּם וְחַנּוּן יְהוָה אֶרֶךְ

to our sins, nor has He repaid us according to our iniquities. 11. For, as the height of the heavens over the earth, so great is His kindness toward those who fear Him. 12. As the distance of east from west, He distanced our transgressions from us. 13. As a father has mercy on sons, the Lord had mercy on those who fear Him. 14. For He knows our creation; He remembers that we are dust. 15. As for man-his days are like grass; like a flower of the field, so does he sprout. 16. For a wind passes over him and he is no longer here; and his place no longer recognizes him. 17. But the Lord's kindness is from everlasting to everlasting, and His charity to sons of sons. 18. To those who keep His covenant and to those who remember His commandments to perform them. 19. The Lord established His throne in the heavens, and His kingdom rules over all. 20. Bless the Lord, His angels, those mighty in strength, who perform His word, to hearken to the voice of His word. 21. Bless the Lord, all His hosts, His ministers, those who do His will. 22. Bless the Lord, all His works, in all the places of His dominion; my soul, bless the Lord.

116

Reflections found on page 118

1. I wished that the Lord would hear my voice [in] my supplications. 2. For He extended His ear to me, and I shall call out in my days. 3. [When] bands of death surrounded me and the boundaries of the grave befell me, and I found trouble and grief, 4. And I called out in the name of the Lord, "Please, O Lord, save my soul! 5. The Lord is gracious and righteous, and our God is merciful. 6. The Lord protects the simple; when I was poor, He saved me. 7. Return, my soul, to your rest, for the Lord has dealt bountifully with you. 8. For You have rescued my soul from death, my eye from tears, and my foot from stumbling. 9. I shall walk before the Lord in the lands of the living. 10. I believed so that I spoke; I humble myself exceedingly. 11. I said in my haste, "All men are liars." 12. How can I repay the Lord for all His favors upon me? 13. I shall lift up a cup of salvations, and I shall call out in the name of the Lord. 14. I shall pay my vows to the Lord now in the presence of all His people. 15. Difficult in the eyes of the Lord is the death of His pious ones. 16. Please, O Lord, for I am Your servant; I am Your servant the son of Your maidservant; You have loosed my thongs. 17. To You I shall slaughter a thanksgiving offering, and I shall call out in the name of the Lord. 18. I shall pay my vows to the Lord

אַפַּיִם וְרַב־חָסֶד׃ ט לֹא־לָנֶצַח יָרִיב וְלֹא לְעוֹלָם יִטּוֹר׃ י לֹא
כַחֲטָאֵינוּ עָשָׂה לָנוּ וְלֹא כַעֲוֹנֹתֵינוּ גָּמַל עָלֵינוּ׃ יא כִּי כִגְבֹהַּ
שָׁמַיִם עַל־הָאָרֶץ גָּבַר חַסְדּוֹ עַל־יְרֵאָיו׃ יב כִּרְחֹק מִזְרָח
מִמַּעֲרָב הִרְחִיק מִמֶּנּוּ אֶת־פְּשָׁעֵינוּ׃ יג כְּרַחֵם אָב עַל־בָּנִים
רִחַם יְהוָה עַל־יְרֵאָיו׃ יד כִּי הוּא יָדַע יִצְרֵנוּ זָכוּר כִּי־עָפָר
אֲנָחְנוּ׃ טו אֱנוֹשׁ כֶּחָצִיר יָמָיו כְּצִיץ הַשָּׂדֶה כֵּן יָצִיץ׃ טז
כִּי רוּחַ עָבְרָה־בּוֹ וְאֵינֶנּוּ וְלֹא־יַכִּירֶנּוּ עוֹד מְקוֹמוֹ׃ יז וְחֶסֶד
יְהוָה ׀ מֵעוֹלָם וְעַד־עוֹלָם עַל־יְרֵאָיו וְצִדְקָתוֹ לִבְנֵי בָנִים׃ יח
לְשֹׁמְרֵי בְרִיתוֹ וּלְזֹכְרֵי פִקֻּדָיו לַעֲשׂוֹתָם׃ יט יְהוָה בַּשָּׁמַיִם
הֵכִין כִּסְאוֹ וּמַלְכוּתוֹ בַּכֹּל מָשָׁלָה׃ כ בָּרֲכוּ יְהוָה מַלְאָכָיו
גִּבֹּרֵי כֹחַ עֹשֵׂי דְבָרוֹ לִשְׁמֹעַ בְּקוֹל דְּבָרוֹ׃ כא בָּרֲכוּ יְהוָה כָּל־
צְבָאָיו מְשָׁרְתָיו עֹשֵׂי רְצוֹנוֹ׃ כב בָּרֲכוּ יְהוָה ׀ כָּל־מַעֲשָׂיו
בְּכָל־מְקֹמוֹת מֶמְשַׁלְתּוֹ בָּרֲכִי נַפְשִׁי אֶת־יְהוָה׃

קטז

א אָהַבְתִּי כִּי־יִשְׁמַע ׀ יְהוָה אֶת־קוֹלִי
תַּחֲנוּנָי׃ ב כִּי־הִטָּה אָזְנוֹ לִי וּבְיָמַי אֶקְרָא׃ ג אֲפָפוּנִי ׀
חֶבְלֵי־מָוֶת וּמְצָרֵי שְׁאוֹל מְצָאוּנִי צָרָה וְיָגוֹן אֶמְצָא׃ ד
וּבְשֵׁם־יְהוָה אֶקְרָא אָנָּה יְהוָה מַלְּטָה נַפְשִׁי׃ ה חַנּוּן יְהוָה
וְצַדִּיק וֵאלֹהֵינוּ מְרַחֵם׃ ו שֹׁמֵר פְּתָאיִם יְהוָה דַּלֹּתִי וְלִי
יְהוֹשִׁיעַ׃ ז שׁוּבִי נַפְשִׁי לִמְנוּחָיְכִי כִּי יְהוָה גָּמַל עָלָיְכִי׃ ח
כִּי חִלַּצְתָּ נַפְשִׁי מִמָּוֶת אֶת־עֵינִי מִן־דִּמְעָה אֶת־רַגְלִי מִדֶּחִי׃
ט אֶתְהַלֵּךְ לִפְנֵי יְהוָה בְּאַרְצוֹת הַחַיִּים׃ י הֶאֱמַנְתִּי כִּי
אֲדַבֵּר אֲנִי עָנִיתִי מְאֹד׃ יא אֲנִי אָמַרְתִּי בְחָפְזִי כָּל־הָאָדָם
כֹּזֵב׃ יב מָה־אָשִׁיב לַיהוָה כָּל־תַּגְמוּלוֹהִי עָלָי׃ יג כּוֹס־
יְשׁוּעוֹת אֶשָּׂא וּבְשֵׁם יְהוָה אֶקְרָא׃ יד נְדָרַי לַיהוָה אֲשַׁלֵּם
נֶגְדָה־נָּא לְכָל־עַמּוֹ׃ טו יָקָר בְּעֵינֵי יְהוָה הַמָּוְתָה לַחֲסִידָיו׃
טז אָנָּה יְהוָה כִּי־אֲנִי עַבְדֶּךָ אֲנִי עַבְדְּךָ בֶּן־אֲמָתֶךָ פִּתַּחְתָּ

now in the presence of all His people, 19. In the courtyards of the house of the Lord, in your midst, O Jerusalem. Hallelujah!

118

Reflections found on page 122

1. Give thanks to the Lord because He is good, for His kindness is eternal. 2. Israel shall now say, "For His kindness is eternal." 3. The house of Aaron shall now say, "For His kindness is eternal." 4. Those who fear the Lord shall now say, "For His kindness is eternal." 5. From the straits I called God; God answered me with a vast expanse. 6. The Lord is for me; I shall not fear. What can man do to me? 7. The Lord is for me with my helpers, and I shall see [revenge] in my enemies. 8. It is better to take shelter in the Lord than to trust in man. 9. It is better to take shelter in the Lord than to trust in princes. 10. All nations surrounded me; in the name of the Lord that I shall cut them off. 11. They encircled me, yea they surrounded me; in the name of the Lord that I shall cut them off. 12. They encircled me like bees; they were extinguished like a thorn fire; in the name of the Lord that I shall cut them off. 13. You pushed me to fall, but the Lord helped me. 14. The might and the cutting power of God was my salvation. 15. A voice of singing praises and salvation is in the tents of the righteous; the right hand of the Lord deals valiantly. 16. The right hand of the Lord is exalted; the right hand of the Lord deals valiantly. 17. I shall not die but I shall live and tell the deeds of God. 18. God has chastised me, but He has not delivered me to death. 19. Open for me the gates of righteousness; I shall enter them and thank God. 20. This is the Lord's gate; the righteous will enter therein. 21. I shall thank You because You answered me, and You were my salvation. 22. The stone that the builders rejected became a cornerstone. 23. This was from the Lord; it is wondrous in our eyes. 24. This is the day that the Lord made; we shall exult and rejoice thereon. 25. Please, O Lord, save now! Please, O Lord, make prosperous now! 26. Blessed be he who has come in the name of the Lord; we have blessed you in the name of the Lord. 27. The Lord is God, and He gave us light. Bind the sacrifice with ropes until [it is brought to] the corners of the altar. 28. You are my God and I shall thank You; the God of my father, and I shall exalt You. 29. Give thanks to the Lord because He is good, for His kindness is eternal.

לְמוֹסֵרָי׃ יז לְךָ־אֶזְבַּח זֶבַח תּוֹדָה וּבְשֵׁם יְהֹוָה אֶקְרָא׃ יח
נְדָרַי לַיהֹוָה אֲשַׁלֵּם נֶגְדָה־נָּא לְכָל־עַמּוֹ׃ יט בְּחַצְרוֹת | בֵּית
יְהֹוָה בְּתוֹכֵכִי יְרוּשָׁלָ͏ִם הַלְלוּיָהּ׃

קיח

א הוֹדוּ לַיהֹוָה כִּי־טוֹב כִּי לְעוֹלָם חַסְדּוֹ׃
ב יֹאמַר־נָא יִשְׂרָאֵל כִּי לְעוֹלָם חַסְדּוֹ׃ ג יֹאמְרוּ נָא בֵית־
אַהֲרֹן כִּי לְעוֹלָם חַסְדּוֹ׃ ד יֹאמְרוּ נָא יִרְאֵי יְהֹוָה כִּי לְעוֹלָם
חַסְדּוֹ׃ ה מִן־הַמֵּצַר קָרָאתִי יָּהּ עָנָנִי בַמֶּרְחָב יָהּ׃ ו יְהֹוָה
לִי לֹא אִירָא מַה־יַּעֲשֶׂה לִי אָדָם׃ ז יְהֹוָה לִי בְּעֹזְרָי וַאֲנִי
אֶרְאֶה בְשֹׂנְאָי׃ ח טוֹב לַחֲסוֹת בַּיהֹוָה מִבְּטֹחַ בָּאָדָם׃ ט
טוֹב לַחֲסוֹת בַּיהֹוָה מִבְּטֹחַ בִּנְדִיבִים׃ י כָּל־גּוֹיִם סְבָבוּנִי
בְּשֵׁם יְהֹוָה כִּי אֲמִילַם׃ יא סַבּוּנִי גַם־סְבָבוּנִי בְּשֵׁם יְהֹוָה
כִּי אֲמִילַם׃ יב סַבּוּנִי כִדְבוֹרִים דֹּעֲכוּ כְּאֵשׁ קוֹצִים בְּשֵׁם
יְהֹוָה כִּי אֲמִילַם׃ יג דַּחֹה דְחִיתַנִי לִנְפֹּל וַיהֹוָה עֲזָרָנִי׃ יד
עָזִּי וְזִמְרָת יָהּ וַיְהִי־לִי לִישׁוּעָה׃ טו קוֹל | רִנָּה וִישׁוּעָה
בְּאָהֳלֵי צַדִּיקִים יְמִין יְהֹוָה עֹשָׂה חָיִל׃ טז יְמִין יְהֹוָה
רוֹמֵמָה יְמִין יְהֹוָה עֹשָׂה חָיִל׃ יז לֹא אָמוּת כִּי־אֶחְיֶה
וַאֲסַפֵּר מַעֲשֵׂי יָהּ׃ יח יַסֹּר יִסְּרַנִּי יָּהּ וְלַמָּוֶת לֹא נְתָנָנִי׃
יט פִּתְחוּ־לִי שַׁעֲרֵי־צֶדֶק אָבֹא־בָם אוֹדֶה יָהּ׃ כ זֶה־הַשַּׁעַר
לַיהֹוָה צַדִּיקִים יָבֹאוּ בוֹ׃ כא אוֹדְךָ כִּי עֲנִיתָנִי וַתְּהִי־לִי
לִישׁוּעָה׃ כב אֶבֶן מָאֲסוּ הַבּוֹנִים הָיְתָה לְרֹאשׁ פִּנָּה׃ כג
מֵאֵת יְהֹוָה הָיְתָה זֹּאת הִיא נִפְלָאת בְּעֵינֵינוּ׃ כד זֶה־הַיּוֹם
עָשָׂה יְהֹוָה נָגִילָה וְנִשְׂמְחָה בוֹ׃ כה אָנָּא יְהֹוָה הוֹשִׁיעָה
נָּא אָנָּא יְהֹוָה הַצְלִיחָה נָּא׃ כו בָּרוּךְ הַבָּא בְּשֵׁם יְהֹוָה
בֵּרַכְנוּכֶם מִבֵּית יְהֹוָה׃ כז אֵל | יְהֹוָה וַיָּאֶר לָנוּ אִסְרוּ־חַג
בַּעֲבֹתִים עַד קַרְנוֹת הַמִּזְבֵּחַ׃ כח אֵלִי אַתָּה וְאוֹדֶךָּ אֱלֹהַי
אֲרוֹמְמֶךָּ׃ כט הוֹדוּ לַיהֹוָה כִּי־טוֹב כִּי לְעוֹלָם חַסְדּוֹ׃

119

Reflections found on page 126

1. Praiseworthy are those whose way is perfect, who walk with the law of the Lord. 2. Praiseworthy are those who keep His testimonies; who seek Him wholeheartedly. 3. Not only have they committed no injustice, they walked in His ways. 4. You commanded Your precepts, to keep diligently. 5. My prayers are that my ways should be established, to keep Your statutes. 6. Then I shall not be ashamed when I look at all Your commandments. 7. I shall thank You with an upright heart when I learn the judgments of Your righteousness. 8. I shall keep Your statutes; do not forsake me utterly. 9. In what manner should a youth purify his way? To observe according to Your word. 10. With all my heart I searched for You; do not cause me to stray from Your commandments. 11. In my heart I hid Your word, in order that I should not sin against You. 12. Blessed are You, O Lord; teach me Your statutes. 13. With my lips I recited all the judgments of Your mouth. 14. With the way of Your testimonies I rejoiced as over all riches. 15. Concerning Your precepts I shall converse, and I shall look at Your ways. 16. With Your statutes I shall occupy myself; I shall not forget Your speech. 17. Bestow kindness upon Your servant; I shall live and I shall keep Your word. 18. Uncover my eyes and I shall look at hidden things from Your Torah. 19. I am a stranger in the land; do not hide Your commandments from me. 20. My soul is crushed from longing for Your judgments at all times. 21. You shall rebuke cursed willful sinners who stray from Your commandments. 22. Remove from me disgrace and contempt, for I kept Your testimonies. 23. Although princes sat and talked about me, Your servant conversed about Your statutes. 24. Also, Your testimonies are my affairs, men of my counsel. 25. My soul clung to the dust; revive me according to Your word. 26. I told of my ways, and You answered me; teach me Your statutes. 27. Make me understand Your precepts, and I shall speak of Your wonders. 28. My soul drips from grief; sustain me according to Your word. 29. Remove from me the way of falsehood, and favor me with Your Torah. 30. I chose the way of faith; Your judgments I have set [before me]. 31. I clung to Your testimonies; O Lord; put me not to shame. 32. [In] the way of Your commandments I shall run, for You will broaden my understanding. 33. Instruct me, O Lord, [in] the way of Your statutes, and I shall keep it at every step. 34. Enable me to understand and I shall keep Your Torah, and I shall keep it wholeheartedly. 35. Lead me in the path of Your commandments for I desired it. 36. Extend my heart to Your testimonies and not to monetary gain. 37. Turn away my eyes from seeing vanity; with Your ways sustain me. 38. Fulfill for Your

קיט

א אַשְׁרֵי תְמִימֵי־דָרֶךְ הַהֹלְכִים בְּתוֹרַת
יְהֹוָה׃ ב אַשְׁרֵי נֹצְרֵי עֵדֹתָיו בְּכָל־לֵב יִדְרְשׁוּהוּ׃ ג אַף לֹא־
פָעֲלוּ עַוְלָה בִּדְרָכָיו הָלָכוּ׃ ד אַתָּה צִוִּיתָה פִקֻּדֶיךָ לִשְׁמֹר
מְאֹד׃ ה אַחֲלַי יִכֹּנוּ דְרָכָי לִשְׁמֹר חֻקֶּיךָ׃ ו אָז לֹא־אֵבוֹשׁ
בְּהַבִּיטִי אֶל־כָּל־מִצְוֹתֶיךָ׃ ז אוֹדְךָ בְּיֹשֶׁר לֵבָב בְּלָמְדִי
מִשְׁפְּטֵי צִדְקֶךָ׃ ח אֶת־חֻקֶּיךָ אֶשְׁמֹר אַל־תַּעַזְבֵנִי עַד־מְאֹד׃
ט בַּמֶּה יְזַכֶּה־נַּעַר אֶת־אָרְחוֹ לִשְׁמֹר כִּדְבָרֶךָ׃ י בְּכָל־לִבִּי
דְרַשְׁתִּיךָ אַל־תַּשְׁגֵּנִי מִמִּצְוֹתֶיךָ׃ יא בְּלִבִּי צָפַנְתִּי אִמְרָתֶךָ
לְמַעַן לֹא אֶחֱטָא־לָךְ׃ יב בָּרוּךְ אַתָּה יְהֹוָה לַמְּדֵנִי חֻקֶּיךָ׃
יג בִּשְׂפָתַי סִפַּרְתִּי כֹּל מִשְׁפְּטֵי־פִיךָ׃ יד בְּדֶרֶךְ עֵדְוֹתֶיךָ
שַׂשְׂתִּי כְּעַל כָּל־הוֹן׃ טו בְּפִקֻּדֶיךָ אָשִׂיחָה וְאַבִּיטָה
אֹרְחֹתֶיךָ׃ טז בְּחֻקֹּתֶיךָ אֶשְׁתַּעֲשָׁע לֹא אֶשְׁכַּח דְּבָרֶךָ׃ יז
גְּמֹל עַל־עַבְדְּךָ אֶחְיֶה וְאֶשְׁמְרָה דְבָרֶךָ׃ יח גַּל־עֵינַי וְאַבִּיטָה
נִפְלָאוֹת מִתּוֹרָתֶךָ׃ יט גֵּר אָנֹכִי בָאָרֶץ אַל־תַּסְתֵּר מִמֶּנִּי
מִצְוֹתֶיךָ׃ כ גָּרְסָה נַפְשִׁי לְתַאֲבָה אֶל־מִשְׁפָּטֶיךָ בְכָל־עֵת׃
כא גָּעַרְתָּ זֵדִים אֲרוּרִים הַשֹּׁגִים מִמִּצְוֹתֶיךָ׃ כב גַּל מֵעָלַי
חֶרְפָּה וָבוּז כִּי עֵדֹתֶיךָ נָצָרְתִּי׃ כג גַּם יָשְׁבוּ שָׂרִים בִּי נִדְבָּרוּ
עַבְדְּךָ יָשִׂיחַ בְּחֻקֶּיךָ׃ כד גַּם־עֵדֹתֶיךָ שַׁעֲשֻׁעַי אַנְשֵׁי עֲצָתִי׃
כה דָּבְקָה לֶעָפָר נַפְשִׁי חַיֵּנִי כִּדְבָרֶךָ׃ כו דְּרָכַי סִפַּרְתִּי
וַתַּעֲנֵנִי לַמְּדֵנִי חֻקֶּיךָ׃ כז דֶּרֶךְ־פִּקּוּדֶיךָ הֲבִינֵנִי וְאָשִׂיחָה
בְּנִפְלְאוֹתֶיךָ׃ כח דָּלְפָה נַפְשִׁי מִתּוּגָה קַיְּמֵנִי כִּדְבָרֶךָ׃ כט
דֶּרֶךְ שֶׁקֶר הָסֵר מִמֶּנִּי וְתוֹרָתְךָ חָנֵּנִי׃ ל דֶּרֶךְ־אֱמוּנָה בָחָרְתִּי
מִשְׁפָּטֶיךָ שִׁוִּיתִי׃ לא דָּבַקְתִּי בְעֵדְוֹתֶיךָ יְהֹוָה אַל־תְּבִישֵׁנִי׃
לב דֶּרֶךְ־מִצְוֹתֶיךָ אָרוּץ כִּי תַרְחִיב לִבִּי׃ לג הוֹרֵנִי יְהֹוָה
דֶּרֶךְ חֻקֶּיךָ וְאֶצְּרֶנָּה עֵקֶב׃ לד הֲבִינֵנִי וְאֶצְּרָה תוֹרָתֶךָ
וְאֶשְׁמְרֶנָּה בְכָל־לֵב׃ לה הַדְרִיכֵנִי בִּנְתִיב מִצְוֹתֶיךָ כִּי בוֹ
חָפָצְתִּי׃ לו הַט־לִבִּי אֶל־עֵדְוֹתֶיךָ וְאַל אֶל־בָּצַע׃ לז הַעֲבֵר
עֵינַי מֵרְאוֹת שָׁוְא בִּדְרָכֶךָ חַיֵּנִי׃ לח הָקֵם לְעַבְדְּךָ אִמְרָתֶךָ

servant Your word that is for Your fear. 39. Remove my disgrace, which I feared, for Your judgments are good. 40. Behold, I longed for Your precepts; with Your righteousness sustain me. 41. And may Your acts of kindness befall me, O Lord, Your salvation according to Your word. 42. And I shall answer a word to those who disgrace me, for I trusted in Your word. 43. And do not take out utterly from my mouth a word of truth, because I hoped for Your words. 44. And I shall keep Your Torah constantly, forever and ever. 45. And I shall walk in widely accepted ways, for I sought Your precepts. 46. And I shall speak of Your testimonies in the presence of kings, and I shall not be ashamed. 47. And I shall engage in Your commandments, which I love. 48. And I shall lift up my palms to your commandments, which I love, and I shall converse about Your statutes. 49. Remember a word to Your servant, through which You gave me hope. 50. This is my consolation in my affliction, for Your word has sustained me. 51. Willful sinners derided me greatly; I did not turn away from Your Torah. 52. I remembered Your judgments of old, O Lord, and I was consoled. 53. Quaking gripped me because of the wicked men who abandoned Your Torah. 54. Your statutes were to me as songs in the house of my sojournings. 55. At night I remembered Your name, O Lord, and I kept Your Torah. 56. This came to me because I kept Your precepts. 57. "The Lord is my portion," I said, to keep Your words. 58. I entreated You with all my heart; favor me according to Your word. 59. I considered my ways, and I returned my feet to Your testimonies. 60. I hastened and did not delay to keep Your commandments. 61. Bands of wicked men robbed me; I did not forget Your Torah. 62. At midnight, I rise to give thanks to You for Your just judgments. 63. I am a companion to all who fear You and to those who keep your precepts. 64. O Lord, the earth is full of Your kindness; teach me Your statutes. 65. You have done good with Your servant, O Lord, according to Your word. 66. The best of reason and knowledge, teach me for I believe in Your commandments. 67. Before I recited, I erred, but now I keep Your word. 68. You are good and You do good; teach me Your statutes. 69. Willful sinners have heaped false accusations upon me, but I keep your precepts wholeheartedly. 70. Thick like fat is their heart, but I engage in Your Torah. 71. It is good for me that I was afflicted, in order that I learn Your statutes. 72. The instruction of Your mouth is better for me than thousands of gold and silver. 73. Your hands made me and fashioned me; enable me to understand, and I shall learn Your commandments. 74. Those who fear You will see me and rejoice for I hoped for Your word. 75. I know, O Lord, that Your judgments are just, and in faith You afflicted me. 76. May Your kindness be [upon me] now to comfort me, as Your word to Your servant. 77. May Your mercy come upon me so that I shall live, for

אֲשֶׁר לְיִרְאָתֶךָ׃ לט הַעֲבֵר חֶרְפָּתִי אֲשֶׁר יָגֹרְתִּי כִּי מִשְׁפָּטֶיךָ
טוֹבִים׃ מ הִנֵּה תָּאַבְתִּי לְפִקֻּדֶיךָ בְּצִדְקָתְךָ חַיֵּנִי׃ מא
וִיבֹאֻנִי חֲסָדֶךָ יְהוָה תְּשׁוּעָתְךָ כְּאִמְרָתֶךָ׃ מב וְאֶעֱנֶה חֹרְפִי
דָבָר כִּי־בָטַחְתִּי בִּדְבָרֶךָ׃ מג וְאַל־תַּצֵּל מִפִּי דְבַר־אֱמֶת עַד־
מְאֹד כִּי לְמִשְׁפָּטֶךָ יִחָלְתִּי׃ מד וְאֶשְׁמְרָה תוֹרָתְךָ תָמִיד
לְעוֹלָם וָעֶד׃ מה וְאֶתְהַלְּכָה בָרְחָבָה כִּי פִקֻּדֶיךָ דָרָשְׁתִּי׃
מו וַאֲדַבְּרָה בְעֵדֹתֶיךָ נֶגֶד מְלָכִים וְלֹא אֵבוֹשׁ׃ מז וְאֶשְׁתַּעֲשַׁע
בְּמִצְוֹתֶיךָ אֲשֶׁר אָהָבְתִּי׃ מח וְאֶשָּׂא כַפַּי אֶל־מִצְוֹתֶיךָ אֲשֶׁר
אָהָבְתִּי וְאָשִׂיחָה בְחֻקֶּיךָ׃ מט זְכָר־דָּבָר לְעַבְדֶּךָ עַל אֲשֶׁר
יִחַלְתָּנִי׃ נ זֹאת נֶחָמָתִי בְעָנְיִי כִּי אִמְרָתְךָ חִיָּתְנִי׃ נא זֵדִים
הֱלִיצֻנִי עַד־מְאֹד מִתּוֹרָתְךָ לֹא נָטִיתִי׃ נב זָכַרְתִּי מִשְׁפָּטֶיךָ
מֵעוֹלָם ׀ יְהוָה וָאֶתְנֶחָם׃ נג זַלְעָפָה אֲחָזַתְנִי מֵרְשָׁעִים
עֹזְבֵי תּוֹרָתֶךָ׃ נד זְמִרוֹת הָיוּ־לִי חֻקֶּיךָ בְּבֵית מְגוּרָי׃ נה
זָכַרְתִּי בַלַּיְלָה שִׁמְךָ יְהוָה וָאֶשְׁמְרָה תּוֹרָתֶךָ׃ נו זֹאת
הָיְתָה־לִּי כִּי פִקֻּדֶיךָ נָצָרְתִּי׃ נז חֶלְקִי יְהוָה אָמַרְתִּי לִשְׁמֹר
דְּבָרֶיךָ׃ נח חִלִּיתִי פָנֶיךָ בְכָל־לֵב חָנֵּנִי כְּאִמְרָתֶךָ׃ נט
חִשַּׁבְתִּי דְרָכָי וָאָשִׁיבָה רַגְלַי אֶל־עֵדֹתֶיךָ׃ ס חַשְׁתִּי וְלֹא
הִתְמַהְמָהְתִּי לִשְׁמֹר מִצְוֹתֶיךָ׃ סא חֶבְלֵי רְשָׁעִים עִוְּדֻנִי
תּוֹרָתְךָ לֹא שָׁכָחְתִּי׃ סב חֲצוֹת־לַיְלָה אָקוּם לְהוֹדוֹת לָךְ
עַל מִשְׁפְּטֵי צִדְקֶךָ׃ סג חָבֵר אָנִי לְכָל־אֲשֶׁר יְרֵאוּךָ וּלְשֹׁמְרֵי
פִּקּוּדֶיךָ׃ סד חַסְדְּךָ יְהוָה מָלְאָה הָאָרֶץ חֻקֶּיךָ לַמְּדֵנִי׃ סה
טוֹב עָשִׂיתָ עִם־עַבְדְּךָ יְהוָה כִּדְבָרֶךָ׃ סו טוּב טַעַם וָדַעַת
לַמְּדֵנִי כִּי בְמִצְוֹתֶיךָ הֶאֱמָנְתִּי׃ סז טֶרֶם אֶעֱנֶה אֲנִי שֹׁגֵג
וְעַתָּה אִמְרָתְךָ שָׁמָרְתִּי׃ סח טוֹב־אַתָּה וּמֵטִיב לַמְּדֵנִי
חֻקֶּיךָ׃ סט טָפְלוּ עָלַי שֶׁקֶר זֵדִים אֲנִי בְּכָל־לֵב ׀ אֶצֹּר
פִּקּוּדֶיךָ׃ ע טָפַשׁ כַּחֵלֶב לִבָּם אֲנִי תּוֹרָתְךָ שִׁעֲשָׁעְתִּי׃ עא
טוֹב־לִי כִי־עֻנֵּיתִי לְמַעַן אֶלְמַד חֻקֶּיךָ׃ עב טוֹב־לִי תוֹרַת
פִּיךָ מֵאַלְפֵי זָהָב וָכָסֶף׃ עג יָדֶיךָ עָשׂוּנִי וַיְכוֹנְנוּנִי הֲבִינֵנִי
וְאֶלְמְדָה מִצְוֹתֶיךָ׃ עד יְרֵאֶיךָ יִרְאוּנִי וְיִשְׂמָחוּ כִּי לִדְבָרְךָ
יִחָלְתִּי׃ עה יָדַעְתִּי יְהוָה כִּי־צֶדֶק מִשְׁפָּטֶיךָ וֶאֱמוּנָה עִנִּיתָנִי׃

Your Torah is my occupation. 78. May the willful sinners be shamed for they condemned me falsely; I shall converse about Your precepts. 79. May those who fear You and those who know Your testimonies return to me. 80. May my heart be perfect in Your statutes in order that I not be shamed. 81. My soul pines for Your salvation; for Your word I hope. 82. My eyes pine for Your word, saying, "When will You console me?" 83. For I have become like a wineskin in smoke; I have not forgotten Your statutes. 84. How many are Your servant's days? When will You execute judgments upon my pursuers? 85. Willful sinners have dug pits for me, which is not according to Your Torah. 86. All Your commandments are faithful; they pursued me in vain; help me. 87. They almost destroyed me on earth, but I did not forsake Your precepts. 88. According to Your kindness, sustain me, and I shall keep the testimony of Your mouth. 89. Forever, O Lord, Your word stands in the heavens. 90. Your faith is to every generation; You established the earth and it endures. 91. For Your judgments they stand today, for all are Your servants. 92. Were not Your Torah my occupation, then I would have perished in my affliction. 93. I shall never forget Your precepts for through them You have sustained me. 94. I am Yours; save me for I sought Your precepts. 95. Concerning me: the wicked hoped to destroy me; I shall ponder Your testimonies. 96. Of every finite thing I have seen the end; Your commandments are very broad. 97. How I love Your Torah! All day it is my conversation. 98. Each of Your commandments makes me wiser than my enemies, for it is always mine. 99. From all my teachers I gained understanding, for Your testimonies are my conversation. 100. From the wise elders I gain understanding, for I kept Your precepts. 101. From every evil way I restrained my feet in order that I keep Your word. 102. From Your judgments I did not turn away, for You guided me. 103. How sweet are Your words to my palate, more than honey to my mouth! 104. From Your precepts I shall gain understanding; therefore, I hate all ways of falsehood. 105. Your words are a lamp for my foot, and light for my path. 106. I swore and I fulfilled, to keep the judgments of Your righteousness. 107. I have been exceedingly humbled; O Lord, sustain me according to Your word. 108. The freewill offerings of my mouth accept now, O Lord, and teach me Your judgments. 109. My soul is constantly in my hand, and I have not forgotten Your Torah. 110. The wicked laid a snare for me, but I did not stray from Your precepts. 111. I inherited Your testimonies forever, for they are the joy of my heart. 112. I have inclined my heart to perform Your statutes forever on their paths. 113. I hate those who harbor iniquitous thoughts, but Your Torah I love. 114. You are my protection and my shield; I hoped for Your word. 115. Go away from me, you evildoers, and I shall keep the commandments of my God. 116.

עו יְהִי־נָא חַסְדְּךָ לְנַחֲמֵנִי כְּאִמְרָתְךָ לְעַבְדֶּךָ׃ עז יְבֹאוּנִי
רַחֲמֶיךָ וְאֶחְיֶה כִּי תוֹרָתְךָ שַׁעֲשֻׁעָי׃ עח יֵבֹשׁוּ זֵדִים כִּי־שֶׁקֶר
עִוְּתוּנִי אֲנִי אָשִׂיחַ בְּפִקּוּדֶיךָ׃ עט יָשׁוּבוּ־לִי יְרֵאֶיךָ וְיֹדְעוּ
[וְיֹדְעֵי] עֵדֹתֶיךָ׃ פ יְהִי־לִבִּי תָמִים בְּחֻקֶּיךָ לְמַעַן לֹא אֵבוֹשׁ׃
פא כָּלְתָה לִתְשׁוּעָתְךָ נַפְשִׁי לִדְבָרְךָ יִחָלְתִּי׃ פב כָּלוּ עֵינַי
לְאִמְרָתֶךָ לֵאמֹר מָתַי תְּנַחֲמֵנִי׃ פג כִּי־הָיִיתִי כְּנֹאד בְּקִיטוֹר
חֻקֶּיךָ לֹא שָׁכָחְתִּי׃ פד כַּמָּה יְמֵי עַבְדֶּךָ מָתַי תַּעֲשֶׂה בְרֹדְפַי
מִשְׁפָּט׃ פה כָּרוּ־לִי זֵדִים שִׁיחוֹת אֲשֶׁר לֹא כְתוֹרָתֶךָ׃ פו
כָּל־מִצְוֹתֶיךָ אֱמוּנָה שֶׁקֶר רְדָפוּנִי עָזְרֵנִי׃ פז כִּמְעַט כִּלּוּנִי
בָאָרֶץ וַאֲנִי לֹא־עָזַבְתִּי פִקֻּדֶיךָ׃ פח כְּחַסְדְּךָ חַיֵּנִי וְאֶשְׁמְרָה
עֵדוּת פִּיךָ׃ פט לְעוֹלָם יְהוָה דְּבָרְךָ נִצָּב בַּשָּׁמָיִם׃ צ לְדֹר
וָדֹר אֱמוּנָתֶךָ כּוֹנַנְתָּ אֶרֶץ וַתַּעֲמֹד׃ צא לְמִשְׁפָּטֶיךָ עָמְדוּ
הַיּוֹם כִּי הַכֹּל עֲבָדֶיךָ׃ צב לוּלֵי תוֹרָתְךָ שַׁעֲשֻׁעָי אָז אָבַדְתִּי
בְעָנְיִי׃ צג לְעוֹלָם לֹא־אֶשְׁכַּח פִּקּוּדֶיךָ כִּי־בָם חִיִּיתָנִי׃ צד
לְךָ־אֲנִי הוֹשִׁיעֵנִי כִּי פִקּוּדֶיךָ דָרָשְׁתִּי׃ צה לִי קִוּוּ רְשָׁעִים
לְאַבְּדֵנִי עֵדֹתֶיךָ אֶתְבּוֹנָן׃ צו לְכָל תִּכְלָה רָאִיתִי קֵץ רְחָבָה
מִצְוָתְךָ מְאֹד׃ צז מָה־אָהַבְתִּי תוֹרָתֶךָ כָּל־הַיּוֹם הִיא
שִׂיחָתִי׃ צח מֵאֹיְבַי תְּחַכְּמֵנִי מִצְוֹתֶךָ כִּי לְעוֹלָם הִיא־לִי׃
צט מִכָּל־מְלַמְּדַי הִשְׂכַּלְתִּי כִּי עֵדְוֹתֶיךָ שִׂיחָה לִי׃ ק מִזְּקֵנִים
אֶתְבּוֹנָן כִּי פִקּוּדֶיךָ נָצָרְתִּי׃ קא מִכָּל־אֹרַח רָע כָּלִאתִי רַגְלָי
לְמַעַן אֶשְׁמֹר דְּבָרֶךָ׃ קב מִמִּשְׁפָּטֶיךָ לֹא־סָרְתִּי כִּי־אַתָּה
הוֹרֵתָנִי׃ קג מַה־נִּמְלְצוּ לְחִכִּי אִמְרָתֶךָ מִדְּבַשׁ לְפִי׃ קד
מִפִּקּוּדֶיךָ אֶתְבּוֹנָן עַל־כֵּן שָׂנֵאתִי ׀ כָּל־אֹרַח שָׁקֶר׃ קה נֵר־
לְרַגְלִי דְבָרֶךָ וְאוֹר לִנְתִיבָתִי׃ קו נִשְׁבַּעְתִּי וָאֲקַיֵּמָה לִשְׁמֹר
מִשְׁפְּטֵי צִדְקֶךָ׃ קז נַעֲנֵיתִי עַד־מְאֹד יְהוָה חַיֵּנִי כִדְבָרֶךָ׃
קח נִדְבוֹת פִּי רְצֵה־נָא יְהוָה וּמִשְׁפָּטֶיךָ לַמְּדֵנִי׃ קט נַפְשִׁי
בְכַפִּי תָמִיד וְתוֹרָתְךָ לֹא שָׁכָחְתִּי׃ קי נָתְנוּ רְשָׁעִים פַּח לִי
וּמִפִּקּוּדֶיךָ לֹא תָעִיתִי׃ קיא נָחַלְתִּי עֵדְוֹתֶיךָ לְעוֹלָם כִּי־
שְׂשׂוֹן לִבִּי הֵמָּה׃ קיב נָטִיתִי לִבִּי לַעֲשׂוֹת חֻקֶּיךָ לְעוֹלָם
עֵקֶב׃ קיג סֵעֲפִים שָׂנֵאתִי וְתוֹרָתְךָ אָהָבְתִּי׃ קיד סִתְרִי

Support me as Your word, and I shall live, and do not put me to shame because of my hope. 117. Sustain me and I shall be saved, and I shall constantly engage in Your statutes. 118. You trampled all who stray from Your statutes, for their deceit is false. 119. As dross, You cut off all the wicked of the earth; therefore I love Your testimonies. 120. My flesh bristles from fear of You, and I dread Your judgments. 121. I performed justice and righteousness; do not leave me to my oppressors. 122. Be surety for Your servant for good; let the willful sinners not oppress me. 123. My eyes pined for Your salvation and for the word of Your righteousness. 124. Deal with Your servant according to Your kindness, and teach me Your statutes. 125. I am Your servant; enable me to understand, and I shall know Your testimonies. 126. A time to do for the Lord; they have made void Your Torah. 127. Because I loved Your commandments more than gold, even more than fine gold. 128. Because I considered all precepts of all things upright; [and] every false way I hated. 129. Your testimonies are hidden; therefore, my soul kept them. 130. The commencement of Your words enlightens; You make the simple understand. 131. I opened my mouth and panted because I yearned for Your commandments. 132. Turn to me and favor me as is Your custom with those who love Your name. 133. Prepare my steps with Your word, and do not allow any iniquity to rule over me. 134. Redeem me from the oppression of man, and I shall keep Your precepts. 135. Cause Your countenance to shine upon Your servant and teach me Your statutes. 136. Rivulets of water ran down from my eyes because they did not keep Your Torah. 137. You are righteous, O Lord, and Your judgments are upright. 138. You commanded Your testimonies, [which are] righteousness, and they are exceedingly faithful. 139. My zeal incenses me, for my adversaries have forgotten Your words. 140. Your word is very pure, and Your servant loves it. 141. I am young and despised; I have not forgotten Your precepts. 142. Your righteousness is perpetual righteousness, and Your Torah is true. 143. Distress and anguish have overtaken me; Your commandments are my occupation. 144. The righteousness of Your testimonies is eternal; enable me to understand and I shall live. 145. I called with all my heart; answer me, O Lord; I shall keep Your statutes. 146. I called to You; save me and I shall keep Your testimonies. 147. I arose early, when it was still night, and I cried out; I hoped for Your word. 148. My eyes preceded the watches to speak of Your word. 149. Hearken to my voice according to Your kindness; O Lord, according to Your custom sustain me. 150. Pursuers of lewdness have drawn near; from Your Torah they have distanced themselves. 151. You are near, O Lord, and all Your commandments are true. 152. From before, I knew from Your testimonies, for You established them to [the end of] the world. 153. See

וּמָגִנִּי אָתָּה לִדְבָרְךָ יִחָלְתִּי׃ קטו סוּרוּ מִמֶּנִּי מְרֵעִים
וְאֶצְּרָה מִצְוֺת אֱלֹהָי׃ קטז סָמְכֵנִי כְאִמְרָתְךָ וְאֶחְיֶה וְאַל־
תְּבִישֵׁנִי מִשִּׂבְרִי׃ קיז סְעָדֵנִי וְאִוָּשֵׁעָה וְאֶשְׁעָה בְחֻקֶּיךָ
תָמִיד׃ קיח סָלִיתָ כָּל־שׁוֹגִים מֵחֻקֶּיךָ כִּי־שֶׁקֶר תַּרְמִיתָם׃
קיט סִגִים הִשְׁבַּתָּ כָל־רִשְׁעֵי־אָרֶץ לָכֵן אָהַבְתִּי עֵדֹתֶיךָ׃ קכ
סָמַר מִפַּחְדְּךָ בְשָׂרִי וּמִמִּשְׁפָּטֶיךָ יָרֵאתִי׃ קכא עָשִׂיתִי
מִשְׁפָּט וָצֶדֶק בַּל־תַּנִּיחֵנִי לְעֹשְׁקָי׃ קכב עֲרֹב עַבְדְּךָ לְטוֹב
אַל־יַעַשְׁקֻנִי זֵדִים׃ קכג עֵינַי כָּלוּ לִישׁוּעָתֶךָ וּלְאִמְרַת
צִדְקֶךָ׃ קכד עֲשֵׂה עִם־עַבְדְּךָ כְחַסְדֶּךָ וְחֻקֶּיךָ לַמְּדֵנִי׃ קכה
עַבְדְּךָ אָנִי הֲבִינֵנִי וְאֵדְעָה עֵדֹתֶיךָ׃ קכו עֵת לַעֲשׂוֹת לַיהֹוָה
הֵפֵרוּ תּוֹרָתֶךָ׃ קכז עַל־כֵּן אָהַבְתִּי מִצְוֺתֶיךָ מִזָּהָב וּמִפָּז׃
קכח עַל־כֵּן | כָּל־פִּקּוּדֵי כֹל יִשָּׁרְתִּי כָּל־אֹרַח שֶׁקֶר שָׂנֵאתִי׃
קכט פְּלָאוֹת עֵדְוֺתֶיךָ עַל־כֵּן נְצָרָתַם נַפְשִׁי׃ קל פֵּתַח דְּבָרֶיךָ
יָאִיר מֵבִין פְּתָיִים׃ קלא פִּי־פָעַרְתִּי וָאֶשְׁאָפָה כִּי לְמִצְוֺתֶיךָ
יָאָבְתִּי׃ קלב פְּנֵה־אֵלַי וְחָנֵּנִי כְּמִשְׁפָּט לְאֹהֲבֵי שְׁמֶךָ׃ קלג
פְּעָמַי הָכֵן בְּאִמְרָתֶךָ וְאַל־תַּשְׁלֶט־בִּי כָל־אָוֶן׃ קלד פְּדֵנִי
מֵעֹשֶׁק אָדָם וְאֶשְׁמְרָה פִּקּוּדֶיךָ׃ קלה פָּנֶיךָ הָאֵר בְּעַבְדֶּךָ
וְלַמְּדֵנִי אֶת־חֻקֶּיךָ׃ קלו פַּלְגֵי־מַיִם יָרְדוּ עֵינָי עַל לֹא־שָׁמְרוּ
תוֹרָתֶךָ׃ קלז צַדִּיק אַתָּה יְהֹוָה וְיָשָׁר מִשְׁפָּטֶיךָ׃ קלח
צִוִּיתָ צֶדֶק עֵדֹתֶיךָ וֶאֱמוּנָה מְאֹד׃ קלט צִמְּתַתְנִי קִנְאָתִי
כִּי־שָׁכְחוּ דְבָרֶיךָ צָרָי׃ קמ צְרוּפָה אִמְרָתְךָ מְאֹד וְעַבְדְּךָ
אֲהֵבָהּ׃ קמא צָעִיר אָנֹכִי וְנִבְזֶה פִּקֻּדֶיךָ לֹא שָׁכָחְתִּי׃ קמב
צִדְקָתְךָ צֶדֶק לְעוֹלָם וְתוֹרָתְךָ אֱמֶת׃ קמג צַר־וּמָצוֹק
מְצָאוּנִי מִצְוֺתֶיךָ שַׁעֲשֻׁעָי׃ קמד צֶדֶק עֵדְוֺתֶיךָ לְעוֹלָם
הֲבִינֵנִי וְאֶחְיֶה׃ קמה קָרָאתִי בְכָל־לֵב עֲנֵנִי יְהֹוָה חֻקֶּיךָ
אֶצֹּרָה׃ קמו קְרָאתִיךָ הוֹשִׁיעֵנִי וְאֶשְׁמְרָה עֵדֹתֶיךָ׃ קמז
קִדַּמְתִּי בַנֶּשֶׁף וָאֲשַׁוֵּעָה לִדְבָרֶיךָ [לִדְבָרְךָ] יִחָלְתִּי׃ קמח
קִדְּמוּ עֵינַי אַשְׁמֻרוֹת לָשִׂיחַ בְּאִמְרָתֶךָ׃ קמט קוֹלִי שִׁמְעָה
כְחַסְדֶּךָ יְהֹוָה כְּמִשְׁפָּטֶךָ חַיֵּנִי׃ קנ קָרְבוּ רֹדְפֵי זִמָּה
מִתּוֹרָתְךָ רָחָקוּ׃ קנא קָרוֹב אַתָּה יְהֹוָה וְכָל־מִצְוֺתֶיךָ

my affliction and release me, for I have not forgotten Your Torah. 154. Plead my cause and redeem me; for Your word sustains me. 155. Salvation is far from the wicked, for they did not seek Your statutes. 156. Your mercies, O Lord, are abundant; according to Your custom, sustain me. 157. Many are my pursuers and my adversaries; from Your testimonies I did not turn away. 158. I saw traitors and I quarreled [with them] because they did not keep your word. 159. See that I love Your precepts, O Lord; according to Your kindness, sustain me. 160. The beginning of Your word is true, and each of Your righteous judgments is eternal. 161. Princes pursued me for nothing, but my heart feared Your word. 162. I rejoice over Your word as one who finds great spoil. 163. I hate falsehood, and I abominate [it], I love Your Torah. 164. Seven times a day I praise You for Your righteous judgments. 165. There is abundant peace to those who love Your Torah, and they have no obstacle. 166. I hoped for Your salvation, O Lord, and I performed Your commandments. 167. My soul kept Your testimonies, and I love them exceedingly. 168. I kept Your precepts and Your testimonies, for all my ways are before You. 169. May my song of prayer draw near before You, O Lord; according to Your word, enable me to understand. 170. May my supplication come before You; according to Your word, save me. 171. My lips will utter praise when You teach me Your statutes. 172. My tongue will proclaim Your word, for all Your commandments are righteous. 173. May Your hand be [ready] to help me, for I have chosen Your precepts. 174. I yearned for Your salvation, O Lord, and Your Torah is my occupation. 175. May my soul live and praise You, and may Your judgments help me. 176. I went astray like a lost lamb; seek Your servant, for I did not forget Your commandments.

121

Reflections found on page 130

1. A song for ascents. I shall raise my eyes to the mountains, from where will my help come? 2. My help is from the Lord, the Maker of heaven and earth. 3. He will not allow your foot to falter; Your Guardian will not slumber. 4. Behold the Guardian of Israel will neither slumber nor sleep. 5. The Lord is your Guardian; the Lord is your shadow; [He is] by your right hand. 6. By day, the sun will not smite you, nor will the moon at night. 7. The Lord will guard you from all evil; He will guard your soul. 8. The Lord will guard your going out and your coming in from now and to eternity.

אֱמֶת׃ קנב קֶדֶם יָדַעְתִּי מֵעֵדֹתֶיךָ כִּי לְעוֹלָם יְסַדְתָּם׃ קנג
רְאֵה־עָנְיִי וְחַלְּצֵנִי כִּי־תוֹרָתְךָ לֹא שָׁכָחְתִּי׃ קנד רִיבָה רִיבִי
וּגְאָלֵנִי לְאִמְרָתְךָ חַיֵּנִי׃ קנה רָחוֹק מֵרְשָׁעִים יְשׁוּעָה כִּי־
חֻקֶּיךָ לֹא דָרָשׁוּ׃ קנו רַחֲמֶיךָ רַבִּים ׀ יְהוָה כְּמִשְׁפָּטֶיךָ
חַיֵּנִי׃ קנז רַבִּים רֹדְפַי וְצָרָי מֵעֵדְוֹתֶיךָ לֹא נָטִיתִי׃ קנח
רָאִיתִי בֹגְדִים וָאֶתְקוֹטָטָה אֲשֶׁר אִמְרָתְךָ לֹא שָׁמָרוּ׃ קנט
רְאֵה כִּי־פִקּוּדֶיךָ אָהָבְתִּי יְהוָה כְּחַסְדְּךָ חַיֵּנִי׃ קס רֹאשׁ־
דְּבָרְךָ אֱמֶת וּלְעוֹלָם כָּל־מִשְׁפַּט צִדְקֶךָ׃ קסא שָׂרִים רְדָפוּנִי
חִנָּם וּמִדְּבָרְיךָ [וּמִדְּבָרְךָ] פָּחַד לִבִּי׃ קסב שָׂשׂ אָנֹכִי עַל־
אִמְרָתֶךָ כְּמוֹצֵא שָׁלָל רָב׃ קסג שֶׁקֶר שָׂנֵאתִי וַאֲתַעֵבָה
תּוֹרָתְךָ אָהָבְתִּי׃ קסד שֶׁבַע בַּיּוֹם הִלַּלְתִּיךָ עַל מִשְׁפְּטֵי
צִדְקֶךָ׃ קסה שָׁלוֹם רָב לְאֹהֲבֵי תוֹרָתֶךָ וְאֵין לָמוֹ מִכְשׁוֹל׃
קסו שִׂבַּרְתִּי לִישׁוּעָתְךָ יְהוָה וּמִצְוֹתֶיךָ עָשִׂיתִי׃ קסז
שָׁמְרָה נַפְשִׁי עֵדֹתֶיךָ וָאֹהֲבֵם מְאֹד׃ קסח שָׁמַרְתִּי פִקּוּדֶיךָ
וְעֵדֹתֶיךָ כִּי כָל־דְּרָכַי נֶגְדֶּךָ׃ קסט תִּקְרַב רִנָּתִי לְפָנֶיךָ יְהוָה
כִּדְבָרְךָ הֲבִינֵנִי׃ קע תָּבוֹא תְּחִנָּתִי לְפָנֶיךָ כְּאִמְרָתְךָ הַצִּילֵנִי׃
קעא תַּבַּעְנָה שְׂפָתַי תְּהִלָּה כִּי תְלַמְּדֵנִי חֻקֶּיךָ׃ קעב תַּעַן
לְשׁוֹנִי אִמְרָתֶךָ כִּי כָל־מִצְוֹתֶיךָ צֶּדֶק׃ קעג תְּהִי־יָדְךָ לְעָזְרֵנִי
כִּי פִקּוּדֶיךָ בָחָרְתִּי׃ קעד תָּאַבְתִּי לִישׁוּעָתְךָ יְהוָה וְתוֹרָתְךָ
שַׁעֲשֻׁעָי׃ קעה תְּחִי־נַפְשִׁי וּתְהַלְלֶךָּ וּמִשְׁפָּטֶךָ יַעֲזְרֻנִי׃ קעו
תָּעִיתִי כְּשֶׂה אֹבֵד בַּקֵּשׁ עַבְדֶּךָ כִּי מִצְוֹתֶיךָ לֹא שָׁכָחְתִּי׃

קכא

שִׁיר לַמַּעֲלוֹת אֶשָּׂא עֵינַי אֶל־הֶהָרִים
מֵאַיִן יָבֹא עֶזְרִי׃ ב עֶזְרִי מֵעִם יְהוָה עֹשֵׂה שָׁמַיִם וָאָרֶץ׃
ג אַל־יִתֵּן לַמּוֹט רַגְלֶךָ אַל־יָנוּם שֹׁמְרֶךָ׃ ד הִנֵּה לֹא יָנוּם
וְלֹא יִישָׁן שׁוֹמֵר יִשְׂרָאֵל׃ ה יְהוָה שֹׁמְרֶךָ יְהוָה צִלְּךָ עַל־
יַד יְמִינֶךָ׃ ו יוֹמָם הַשֶּׁמֶשׁ לֹא־יַכֶּכָּה וְיָרֵחַ בַּלָּיְלָה׃ ז יְהוָה
יִשְׁמָרְךָ מִכָּל־רָע יִשְׁמֹר אֶת־נַפְשֶׁךָ׃ ח יְהוָה יִשְׁמָר־צֵאתְךָ
וּבוֹאֶךָ מֵעַתָּה וְעַד־עוֹלָם׃

142

Reflections found on page 134

1. A *Maskil* of David, when he was in the cave, a prayer. 2. [With] my voice, I cry out to the Lord; [with] my voice, I supplicate the Lord. 3. I pour out before Him my speech; my distress I recite before Him. 4. When my spirit enwraps itself upon me, and You know my path. In whichever way I go, they have hidden a snare for me. 5. Looking to the right, I see that no one recognizes me; escape is lost from me; no one seeks my soul. 6. I cried out to You, O Lord; I said, "You are my refuge, my lot in the land of the living." 7. Hearken to my cry for I have become very low; save me from my pursuers for they have overpowered me. 8. Take my soul out of confinement to give thanks to Your name; because of me the righteous will crown You, because You will recompense me.

148

Reflections found on page 138

1. Hallelujah! Praise the Lord from the heavens, praise Him in the heights. 2. Praise Him, all His angels; praise Him, all His hosts. 3. Praise Him, sun and moon; praise Him, all stars of the night. 4. Praise Him, highest heavens and the water that is above the heavens. 5. They shall praise the name of the Lord, for He commanded and they were created. 6. And He set them up to eternity, yea forever, He issued a decree, which will not change. 7. Praise the Lord from the earth, sea monsters and all deeps. 8. Fire and hail, snow and vapor, a storm wind, performing His word. 9. The mountains and all the hills, fruit trees and all cedars. 10. Beasts and all cattle, creeping things and winged fowl. 11. Kings of the earth and all kingdoms, princes and all judges of the earth. 12. Youths and also maidens, old men with young boys, 13. Will praise the name of the Lord, for His name alone is powerful; His splendor is on earth and heaven. 14. He raised up a horn for His people, praise to all His pious ones, to the children of Israel, the people close to Him. Hallelujah!

קמב

א מַשְׂכִּיל לְדָוִד בִּהְיוֹתוֹ בַמְּעָרָה תְפִלָּה׃
ב קוֹלִי אֶל־יְהוָה אֶזְעָק קוֹלִי אֶל־יְהוָה אֶתְחַנָּן׃ ג אֶשְׁפֹּךְ
לְפָנָיו שִׂיחִי צָרָתִי לְפָנָיו אַגִּיד׃ ד בְּהִתְעַטֵּף עָלַי ׀ רוּחִי
וְאַתָּה יָדַעְתָּ נְתִיבָתִי בְּאֹרַח־זוּ אֲהַלֵּךְ טָמְנוּ פַח לִי׃ ה
הַבֵּיט יָמִין ׀ וּרְאֵה וְאֵין־לִי מַכִּיר אָבַד מָנוֹס מִמֶּנִּי אֵין
דּוֹרֵשׁ לְנַפְשִׁי׃ ו זָעַקְתִּי אֵלֶיךָ יְהוָה אָמַרְתִּי אַתָּה מַחְסִי
חֶלְקִי בְּאֶרֶץ הַחַיִּים׃ ז הַקְשִׁיבָה ׀ אֶל־רִנָּתִי כִּי־דַלּוֹתִי
מְאֹד הַצִּילֵנִי מֵרֹדְפַי כִּי אָמְצוּ מִמֶּנִּי׃ ח הוֹצִיאָה מִמַּסְגֵּר ׀
נַפְשִׁי לְהוֹדוֹת אֶת־שְׁמֶךָ בִּי יַכְתִּרוּ צַדִּיקִים כִּי תִגְמֹל עָלָי׃

קמח

א הַלְלוּיָהּ ׀ הַלְלוּ אֶת־יְהוָה מִן־הַשָּׁמַיִם
הַלְלוּהוּ בַּמְּרוֹמִים׃ ב הַלְלוּהוּ כָל־מַלְאָכָיו הַלְלוּהוּ
כָּל־צְבָאָו [צְבָאָיו]׃ ג הַלְלוּהוּ שֶׁמֶשׁ וְיָרֵחַ הַלְלוּהוּ כָּל־
כּוֹכְבֵי אוֹר׃ ד הַלְלוּהוּ שְׁמֵי הַשָּׁמָיִם וְהַמַּיִם אֲשֶׁר ׀ מֵעַל
הַשָּׁמָיִם׃ ה יְהַלְלוּ אֶת־שֵׁם יְהוָה כִּי הוּא צִוָּה וְנִבְרָאוּ׃ ו
וַיַּעֲמִידֵם לָעַד לְעוֹלָם חָק־נָתַן וְלֹא יַעֲבוֹר׃ ז הַלְלוּ אֶת־
יְהוָה מִן־הָאָרֶץ תַּנִּינִים וְכָל־תְּהֹמוֹת׃ ח אֵשׁ וּבָרָד שֶׁלֶג
וְקִיטוֹר רוּחַ סְעָרָה עֹשָׂה דְבָרוֹ׃ ט הֶהָרִים וְכָל־גְּבָעוֹת עֵץ
פְּרִי וְכָל־אֲרָזִים׃ י הַחַיָּה וְכָל־בְּהֵמָה רֶמֶשׂ וְצִפּוֹר כָּנָף׃ יא
מַלְכֵי־אֶרֶץ וְכָל־לְאֻמִּים שָׂרִים וְכָל־שֹׁפְטֵי אָרֶץ׃ יב בַּחוּרִים
וְגַם־בְּתוּלוֹת זְקֵנִים עִם־נְעָרִים׃ יג יְהַלְלוּ ׀ אֶת־שֵׁם יְהוָה
כִּי־נִשְׂגָּב שְׁמוֹ לְבַדּוֹ הוֹדוֹ עַל־אֶרֶץ וְשָׁמָיִם׃ יד וַיָּרֶם קֶרֶן ׀
לְעַמּוֹ תְּהִלָּה לְכָל־חֲסִידָיו לִבְנֵי יִשְׂרָאֵל עַם־קְרֹבוֹ הַלְלוּיָהּ׃